T0196875

City Girl Goes Bush

An Eleven Year Odyssey

Dianne Cramer

BALBOA
PRESS

A DIVISION OF HAY HOUSE

Balboa Press books may be ordered through
booksellers or by contacting:

Balboa Press
A Division of Hay House
1663 Liberty Drive
Bloomington, IN 47403
www.balboapress.com.au
1 (877) 407-4847

Because of the dynamic nature of the Internet, any web
addresses or links contained in this book may have changed
since publication and may no longer be valid. The views
expressed in this work are solely those of the author and do
not necessarily reflect the views of the publisher, and the
publisher hereby disclaims any responsibility for them.

The author of this book does not dispense medical advice or
prescribe the use of any technique as a form of treatment for
physical, emotional, or medical problems without the advice
of a physician, either directly or indirectly. The intent of the
author is only to offer information of a general nature to
help you in your quest for emotional and spiritual well-being.
In the event you use any of the information in this book for
yourself, which is your constitutional right, the author and
the publisher assume no responsibility for your actions.

Any people depicted in stock imagery provided
by Thinkstock are models, and such images are
being used for illustrative purposes only.
Certain stock imagery © Thinkstock.

Print information available on the last page.

ISBN: 978-1-5043-1181-6 (sc)
ISBN: 978-1-5043-1180-9 (e)

Balboa Press rev. date: 02/07/2018

DEDICATION

This book is dedicated to the memory of my amazing husband Colin Dehlis Cramer (1929–2012), and earlier pioneers who ventured into the centre of Australia to make a living under incredible hardships. Some wrote of their experiences in the country previously inhabited by indigenous peoples who lived and thrived there for thousands of years - in desert, grasslands and bush, eating bush fruits, roots, kangaroos, emus, bustards, and other soft-footed animals. Although well intentioned, the new settlers' introduction of cattle, horses, camels, donkeys, pigs, goats, sheep and rabbits quickly degraded the land, forcing many settlers to retreat to 'greener pastures' and opening the way for its previous occupants to return.

ACKNOWLEDGMENTS

The author is deeply indebted to her family and many friends; Ray and Barbara Spencer who encouraged her to prepare the story for print, and then edited and formatted the text so professionally; and Clive Chadder for preparing the maps.

CONTENTS

AUSTRALIA

CENTRAL AUSTRALIA ENLARGEMENT

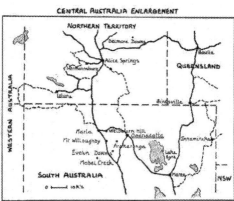

INTRODUCTION

This memoir is my personal recollection, which goes back to a simpler time where we lived without fear or favour; authorities were respected; miles were miles; measurements were yards, feet and inches; and we dealt with pounds, shillings and pence. In a world recovering from war, it was a time when we accepted hardships and drama as part of the fabric of life, which we experienced and then went on to the next phase.

I was 19 years old with a well-paid secure job in Adelaide, but I yearned to live in the country. After a couple of holidays on farms, experiencing country life, I responded to an advertisement, which resulted in my first taste of the outback as governess to an eight-year-old girl on a remote sheep station south-west of Oodnadatta. This was the bush on a grand scale with vast distances and beautiful, rugged landscapes, gorgeous sunsets and raging dust storms.

I met my future husband the day I arrived in Oodnadatta. Then out to the station with the family in a couple of days. I had various adventures on that station, followed by a year in the Northern Territory as governess to two young boys. While there I met some very interesting Territory characters in Alice Springs, celebrated my engagement, and in early 1957 was married in Adelaide. Memories of many different experiences are included in this book where I touch on the hardships and joys of cattle station life - in camp, in shearers' quarters, in a cottage, and in a rambling homestead in the days before good refrigeration, air conditioning and instant communication.

The Royal Flying Doctor Service (RFDS) was paramount in giving us the 'Mantle of Safety' envisioned and put into practice by the Reverend John Flynn of the Inland. The RFDS transceivers were our lifeline, providing communication with folk over an enormous area of South Australia and with medical and telegraphic bases. We knew those folk only by their radio voices – many we never met, but we felt connected to them in a way that was unique. Every station had an airstrip so a small plane could land in cases of emergency.

A land where heat, dust, flies and isolation were the norm, but it was such an interesting way of life, with daily challenges a-plenty. The children grew up tough and the missus was wife, mother, cook, baker, nurse, comforter, assistant, driver, and any other role you can think of.

Indigenous people played a significant role in the cattle industry but changes in Government policy destroyed their camp way-of-life and changed the cattle industry. But it is good to see many of these stations returning to their original conditions and traditional owners, including the Mt Willoughby IPA (Indigenous Protected Area), declared in 2002, being administered from Coober Pedy. Now, more value is placed on the unique flora and fauna, notwithstanding that my family and I spent good years there and have great memories of life on that marginal gibber plain.

We left the bush in the eighth year of a 10-year drought where the country looked dreadful, but was home to us who hold the bush in our hearts.

My wish is that you, the reader, will enjoy the journey with me as I narrate my experiences as closely as I recall.

PART I
THE GOVERNESS

Oodnadatta 1955

Oodnadatta and the Races

The door of the DC3 opened and I walked out onto the steps. The heat struck like a blow after the air-conditioned cabin. Dark red dirt confronted me. Then a man and two small children appeared out of the mirage as I descended the steps. This was my new boss, Dick Holt from Evelyn Downs, holding the hands of Louise, eight, and Ross, three. I was to be Louise's governess, to supervise her Correspondence Course lessons mailed from Adelaide. It was a Saturday in April 1955.

Both children wore green cotton fly-veils to protect their eyes, noses and mouths from the ever-present flies, which were a hazard to small children and adults alike. Yes, it was hot. I was the only passenger to alight, followed by the mailbags and freight, before the plane took off for Alice Springs. I left Adelaide Airport in the early morning and, with a stopover at Leigh Creek, took about five hours to reach Oodnadatta.

After collecting my luggage, we drove into the township and Evelyn Downs' shack where I met Dick's wife, Helen. The shack was a small weekender built to house the family when in town for short stays for whatever reason.

As I later discovered, most outback stations had a shack either in the township or on the east side of the railway line because accommodation was extremely limited, not only for station owners/managers, but also for staff, including housemaids, governesses, station hands, contractors, and visitors.

While various events attracted visitors to the town, there were three major annual events when everyone gathered there: the Oodnadatta races in April, the Australian Inland Mission (AIM) and Royal Flying Doctor Service fund-raising event in September, and a Christmas party in December. I arrived on Saturday during race weekend so, instead of driving to the property immediately, we stayed in the shack for the celebrations where I met various people from the surrounding stations, including young stockmen who were pleased to see some new female blood in town.

1955 Oodnadatta Cup Winner 'Sunspar' Bob & Rona Kempe with John Kemp, Jockey Rollo Severin. Left - Sir George Jenkins. Photo with permission from the Oodnadatta Racing Club

Saturday's main event was the Oodnadatta Cup, which everyone gathered to see. Although the whole set-up was pretty basic, with a makeshift bar under a lean-to shed, everyone enjoyed the get-together. Bob Kempe, of Mt Barry Station, plus a number of other station owners, bred and trained horses for the races.

In the evening, there was a 'races ball' where I met quite a number of young men. What fun. I had never danced before and had quite a time learning how to be led around the floor to the music of a band.

Between dances, the men disappeared outside and returned when the music started again, very much livelier after a few beers! On Sunday afternoon there was a gymkhana that the station hands enjoyed and after the presentations, the race weekend was over.

Arckaringa Homestead 1955

On Monday morning, we cleaned and tidied the shack, then packed up and headed for the station, about 170km south-west of Oodnadatta. Along the way, we drove through the amazing Painted Desert, including Mt Battarbee named after artist Rex Battarbee who had painted it some years before, but now called Mt Arckaringa. About 100km from Oodnadatta we called in to see Skipper and Mrs Partridge at Arckaringa homestead.

Skipper and Mrs Partridge

Reverend Kingsley 'Skipper' Partridge, a retired Presbyterian minister from the AIM, and his wife Gertie, were caretaking Arckaringa Station for Mrs Brown of Mt Willoughby Station, who had known them for many years and was a great supporter of their work.

Skipper had been a companion and fellow-worker of Reverend John Flynn, the visionary 'Flynn of the Inland' who created the 'Mantle of Safety' radio network in the outback. Flynn had contracted Alf Traeger in Adelaide to develop the radio transceiver to enable people 'in the bush' to keep in contact with each other and the medical and telegraphic services in Port Augusta, 800km to the south.

John Flynn's first camel padre was Bruce Plowman, whose travels throughout the parish from Oodnadatta to Katharine in the Northern Territory were described in Plowman's book, *The Man from Oodnadatta*.

Australian Inland Mission (AIM) hostels were eventually built in most remote outback towns in Australia, each staffed by two highly qualified nursing sisters who were contracted to give two years' service. Oodnadatta Hostel, built and staffed in 1911, was the first of many.

After Bruce Plowman retired, Skipper became the second camel padre and served in the 1920s, 30s, and 40s, continuing the work of encouraging the early settlers and miners, arranging matters, baptising children, conducting marriages and burials, besides writing letters, installing and repairing transceivers, and a myriad of other duties. Skipper's story is told in his biography *Camel Trains and Aeroplanes: The Story of Skipper Partridge* written by Arch Grant, It is a wonderful read.

Skipper was a quiet man, but very skilled in all manner of bush work. Having grown up on a farm in NSW, he lent a hand to whatever was going on at the stations he visited. His wife, Gertie, was his mainstay and travelled with him after camels were replaced by motor vehicles. Gertie was a trained nurse who filled in for AIM sisters when they took leave or were sick. Skipper and Gertie had a daughter, Grace, who in turn also became a nurse. It was a pleasure to meet them.

Evelyn Downs

From Arckaringa we drove 33km to a little cottage called SM (San Marino), then another 24km south from the Oodnadatta road through very flat claypan country, with spectacular low ranges on the eastern horizon, to reach Evelyn Downs homestead.

Evelyn Downs was a 2,500km² sheep station with fenced paddocks, surrounded by unfenced cattle stations. A small station for this area, it was sustained by good wool prices and good summer rain. The season was very favourable when I arrived, but locusts came along and ate a lot of the feed.

Dick had built a very small lean-to on the back of the homestead for me, their first governess. Until then, Louise's mother had supervised her lessons. My room was about 2.5m square and had a door and a louvre window, but not much else. It definitely wasn't large enough to swing a cat and was hot in summer and cold in winter; it was furnished with a bed, some shelves, and a bench at the foot of the bed.

The homestead itself consisted of two main rooms built of concrete, separated by a wide breezeway and surrounded by a kitchen, bathroom, schoolroom and bedrooms. The two inner rooms, the sitting room, and Dick and Helen's bedroom, were the only rooms with glass windows, except for the bathroom that had glass louvres. The other rooms had openings in their outside walls covered with fly wire and wooden shutters, which made them very dark when closed during dust storms and winter.

The only air-conditioning that homesteads had in those days were 32 volt electric Breezaires, of which there were only two in the house, one in the main bedroom, the other in the children's bedroom. A diesel engine generated power for the house and workshop, which was noisy and expensive to run, so it was always a relief when it was turned off in the evening.

I settled in and surveyed my new surroundings. The only toilet, a chemical one where the lid had to be raised and lowered to circulate the waste, was far away in the corner of the back yard. Like all bush toilets, it stank, but as this was the same everywhere else, I got used to it. Showers, of necessity, had to be quick to avoid wasting water. General household water came from a bore, with rainwater tanks supplying our very precious drinking water.

Correspondence lessons were there for Louise and it didn't take us long to settle in to schoolwork; she was a quiet, amenable little girl.

Then a surprise - one of the blokes I'd met at the Saturday-night dance turned up; it was Colin Cramer, a station hand from Mt Willoughby, the neighbouring cattle station. Over the next couple of days, he brought a sedan car, a truck and a Land Rover to learn mechanics from Dick, an excellent mechanic, and he stayed at Evelyn Downs for the next three and a half months. During that time, he stayed in the men's quarters and joined us for meals. What a great opportunity to get to know this chap.

Who was this blonde, bronzed, blue-eyed bushman?

I digress.....

What I subsequently learned about bushmen was that the stockmen were indispensable assets to the stations in the days when all mustering was done by men on horses equipped with swags, food, and cooking utensils in packs, called 'the plant'. The men worked in all weathers with mobs of cattle, from baking dry heat and dust to cold, wet weather, under a warm Tasmanian Bluey coat.

They were hard men, with hard, calloused hands – gloves? – don't make me laugh; everything was done with bare hands, often with half inch (12mm) thick callouses on the palms.

The men smelled of cattle, leather, tobacco and sweat – but it was a clean cattleman smell; not at all unpleasant. They hated 'tailor-made' cigarettes, choosing to only 'roll your own' with tobacco from two oz. tins ordered by the boxful. If the stores didn't come, they rolled them thinner until the mail truck delivered new supplies to the station, which were then quickly taken miles away to the stock camp.

When required, they mustered wild horses (brumbies) into the homestead yard to select the best looking ones to break in and educate for cattle work. They also made their own greenhide hobble straps, pouches to hold a pocket-knife and watch on their belts, and small saddle-bags to carry personal gear for repairing leather. In the blacksmith's shop, they heated, hammered and shaped the horseshoes before nailing them onto their horses' hooves.

Every camp had a horse tailer responsible for looking after the plant comprising three or four horses for each stockman, that were rotated. The horse tailer was always the first to rise in the morning, usually around 4am, to listen for and then locate the horses from the sound of the bell. Then, either on foot or riding the night horse, they rounded up the horses and brought them into camp. More on that later.

The men were tough, but with a soft heart that appreciated the women in the country. Their diet was mostly salt beef and damper, with onions and potatoes as the only vegetables, sometimes only onions because they carried well, especially in the dry heat. In the extreme heat, potatoes could go rotten.

At night, they made their beds on the ground with a large grey folded blanket on a waterproof canvas sheet; a pillow could be a change of clothes, and perhaps they had a western or book of poetry to read. It wasn't unknown for dingoes to enter a camp during the night and pull out a swag-strap and give it a good chew – but it was usually located in the morning when the swag was rolled and tied at each end with swag straps before being thrown over a pack horse.

They built fences by hand using an axe and saw to cut posts before chainsaws arrived, and a crowbar to dig the post-holes; they could drill for water, raise a windmill and set up a holding tank with accompanying troughs and yards. They could muster and yard cattle all day, rope a steer, brand and castrate calves, then take turns on a two-hour watch at night; and they could make a stew or curry, damper, or johnny cakes over the coals to feed the stock camp.

Johnny cakes you ask? Depending on the number of men in the camp, the cook for the day measured quantities of flour, baking powder and water to mix into a medium (scone) dough from which small handfuls were rolled between the palms, pressed flat, then laid directly onto hot coals until they puffed, then turned over to cook the other side. Johnny cakes were very quick to make and, with ash brushed off and spread with golden syrup or jam, they were delicious.

Groups of stockmen drove mobs of cattle across country without the benefit of a compass and without fail arrived at their planned destinations. Not only could they 'read' the land, they could also 'read' the mood of the mob to determine which beasts were the leaders, which were the tailenders, and which ones would break.

To relax, the men could sit for hours on their haunches in high-heeled riding boots, leaning elbows on knees, with Akubra hat tipped back to reveal an unshaved face. No bushman was ever seen without his bushman's hat, usually pulled low over his eyes.

They could talk with their mates for hours, hopefully tipping a long-neck beer to lubricate their dry throats. The beer was rarely cold, but it quenched the thirst and livened the conversation; the alternative was hot, strong, sweet tea, boiled in a blackened billy over hot coals.

Colin with his blue cattle dog

A bit of Colin's background

Colin went to Mt Willoughby Station in 1947 to work as a stockman/station-hand, having previously lived in the Barossa Valley amongst his extended family before his parents moved him and his two teenage brothers to a five-acre (two hectares) property at Gilles Plains on the outskirts of Adelaide. His Dad (Bill) worked at Islington railway workshops and owned three trotting horses over a period of years - so his sons became accustomed to being outdoors and around horses. In summer, they grew watermelons for the local market.

Colin left school the day he turned 14 – when he was still in Grade 7 at Primary School. Obviously, he wasn't a scholar; children in the 1940s had to pass exams to be promoted to the next class. However, he got a job straight away driving a horse and cart delivering chaff for a local farmer, Mr Lochan, in the northern suburbs of Adelaide and as far west as Port Adelaide. He later moved to Port Lincoln with his older brother Gilbert, where they worked in the S.A. Brush Company factory (SABCO).

The lads loved to go out shooting at weekends to bag kangaroos or rabbits, but after a few months they decided on another change; Colin returned to Adelaide and Gilbert went to a cattle station in Central Australia, then on to Hermannsburg as a contractor for the Hermannsburg mission. There he met Mona Kennedy, a teacher, and they were married with a little toddler, Rodney, when I first met Colin.

Colin's younger brother Ray worked at Farnham's market garden at Paradise, a suburb of Adelaide. His girlfriend was Val Clements.

Even Earlier Cramer History

Colin's dad moved to the Barossa Valley from Victoria where, as a young man, he helped his older brothers set themselves up on farms. He met his wife in the Barossa – a second generation German raised on a farm.

Colin's dad bought a big Clydesdale stallion, which he took to farms in the Barossa Valley to service mares, but because this didn't generate enough income for a family with three young boys, he got another job at Islington Railways workshops. To get there he rode his bike to Gawler on Monday mornings to catch the train to the city, returning home on Friday evenings. When able to do so, Colin's mother worked in the vineyards.

Colin's Dad, Ray and Colin sewing wheat bags. Windsor Hotel in background

The family rented various houses in the district and the boys started school in Tanunda, but they eventually moved to Adelaide to be near Islington where they found a property to rent at Gilles Plains – an old house on five acres out in the wheat fields.

To supplement the family's income, Colin's mother worked in the kitchen at the nearby Windsor Hotel, while Bill and the boys got extra work with local farmers - after school for the boys. Gilbert and Ray had some secondary education but as previously mentioned, Colin left school the day he turned 14, the legal age for leaving school.

When their rented house came up for sale the family bought it, with the mother and three boys paying it off.

That's when Colin's dad had trotters and instilled the hard-working ethic that Colin retained for the rest of his life.

Some of My Family History

My great-grandparents migrated from England in the 1800s and my mother's father owned chaff mills in Gawler and the Adelaide Hills. He built a large home at Gawler, named 'Orange Grove' for obvious reasons, and later bought another big house on the Esplanade at Henley Beach South. They needed a big house to accommodate their large family - my mother was the tenth of eleven children – plus grandparents; both the Gawler and Esplanade houses had self-contained sections to accommodate mum's grandparents who had migrated from Aylesbury, England, as free settlers. So Colin and I both have farming ancestors.

My Dad also worked at Islington as a Stores Officer and eventually learnt where every bit of hardware owned by the South Australian Railways was located. After I married I discovered that he was also a mathematician – but at that time, young people weren't particularly interested in their parents' talents!

During my growing years Dad was transferred to Tailem Bend to take charge of the Railway Stores where we spent five years (1940-1945) living on the edge of town, opposite the sale yards – which my brother and I loved. We then moved to Henley Beach for a short time, and eventually to Prospect where Dad bought a house in the suburbs and my brother and I went to primary and secondary school before gaining employment – my brother in the country and me in the city.

Why did I want to live in Central Australia?

I grew up in a conservative, middle-class home, and received an excellent commercial education before gaining a well-paid job in Adelaide as a shorthand/typist/secretary at the Electricity Trust of South Australia; but I longed to live in the country. After spending two months of 1954 on a dairy farm near Kin Kin in Queensland, followed by two months in a Brisbane office and staying at a YMCA hostel, my parents called me home when my brother had a serious accident.

This time I got a secretarial job in Adelaide with the Caterpillar Tractor Company, but I was chafing at the bit and kept searching advertisements in the daily paper for a country job until I found one for a governess on a sheep station near Oodnadatta. Having no idea of Oodnadatta's location, I looked up the atlas and discovered that it was in the area where I longed to work. So I sent off a letter telling the people all about myself and they immediately sent me a telegram to offer me the job. Unfortunately, I was at work when the telegram arrived and my parents opened it – they were shocked and horrified, and sent a telegram back straight away saying that I would not accept the position, as they knew nothing about my application.

So when I got home there was a great uproar - What was I thinking? Why would I give up an excellent, well-paying office job to go to the outback? With my education, etc., etc., etc. To add to the pain my brother, who had recently returned home from wool-classing in the Broken Hill area, didn't help by describing bush people as a pretty rough lot and saying that he wouldn't recommend I take the job!

Fortunately, the station owners sent a second telegram requesting my parents to contact a particular person in the adjoining Adelaide suburb for reassurance, who Dad immediately recognised from the name and address. As it turned out, Dad grew up just three doors from them in Avenel Gardens Road, Medindie, and his younger sister was a friend of the station owner's older sister. Phew, a sigh of relief, they were good people and I was given the go ahead, although Dad and Mum were still very upset with me; I was thrilled to be going to a family they felt comfortable with!

Back to Evelyn Downs Station

So there I was, installed in my tiny room on this remote station homestead, preparing to supervise an eight-year-old's education using lessons from the Adelaide Correspondence School that arrived every fortnight on the mail truck.

Colin meanwhile was pulling down and re-building the vehicles he had brought from Mt Willoughby. Dick was an excellent teacher and Colin was a good learner, but he had a big problem – he was a dirty worker. Dick never had a spot of grease anywhere on his clothes, but it seemed that whenever Colin approached anything greasy, the grease leapt out and landed on him and his clothes! Regrettably, keeping clean was something Colin never learned from Dick, ever.

The days were busy for everyone and I soon slipped into the routine of bush life and schoolwork with Louise.

What did we do for recreation? There were always long letters to write to the family in Adelaide of new experiences and I have always loved reading, so I was never without something to do. In the evenings, Colin and I played darts or table tennis.

When fresh meat was needed, Dick sent Colin and me out in the ute to locate a flock of sheep for a killer (a sheep chosen for meat, always a wether – a male castrated as a lamb to grow to produce wool for sale and meat for the table). Colin shot then butchered a suitable one, which was all very exciting for me, not having experienced anything like it before - but it soon became a familiar part of station life.

Dick was born and reared in Adelaide but had come to the area some years before to take up the station. His first bush home was a bough shed, a simple log frame covered with boughs of foliage, which was cool in summer and cold in winter, but it burnt down – a familiar fate for bush homes in those early days.

Then he built a more substantial house, which he later enlarged when he married Helen and they had children. Helen came from Adelaide in the 1940s as a Land Army girl, a scheme where women volunteered to work on the land to replace the men who had gone to war.

Bough Shed [060913PD from the Badjaling/Winmar collection State Library, Western Australia]

It was very quiet when Colin went back to Mt Willoughby, the 5,200km² cattle station where he was employed as a stockman/station-hand and fencing contractor, but he also put down a number of bores on the station and equipped them with mills, tanks, troughs and holding yards, each with a bronco peg for branding calves.

Fortunately, for me, Dick liked to use every available person to go mustering on horseback and to work in the sheep yards at mulesing and shearing times. So I got a fair bit of extra-curricular work on the property, which I preferred to sitting in the schoolroom, although I enjoyed teaching Louise.

Some weekends I packed a picnic lunch and took the children walking, heading to a clay pan of water after rain about 1.5km from the house where we'd eat our lunch and the children played in the water. I also loved to walk alone along Evelyn Creek, a beautiful big sandy creek lined with gum trees that was a few hundred metres from the house, beyond the shearing-shed and yards.

One day during morning tea, Ross came running into the house saying 'nake, nake', and Dick rushed out to find a little lizard on the path, not a snake at all, thankfully. It gave us all a fright though; we saw very few snakes at Evelyn Downs.

The Evelyn Downs radio transceiver, located in the wide breezeway in the middle of the house, was connected to the Bush Church Aid Society base at Ceduna, with signals received through a 27m aerial out in the yard. Radio reception was vital for every station, being the only means of daily communication with the outside world. Ordinary radio reception from the ABC and commercial stations could be quite erratic, with better signals coming in at night.

There were plenty of visitors during the year, including Dick's mother - a lovely lady who was very proud of her son and his sheep station. Dick's older sister Eileen (the one who had played with my father's younger sister as children) and her husband Russ also came to help with the shearing and provide good company.

On another occasion, we had a 'drop in' aircraft that we all went to see - a Dragon Rapide (VH-AGI) from Ceduna piloted by Alan Chadwick that landed on the station airstrip during an orientation flight to various stations.

With such good rain earlier in the year, Mr Horace Ising, Helen's father and well-known Adelaide botanist, came for an extended time to explore the breakaway country south of the homestead, where he found a new plant species that he named after his daughter. Because he liked to listen to the ABC news, we all had to be quiet every lunch time so that he could hear the world news. However, he was a great help with the annual shearing, returning to Adelaide before the weather got too hot.

Helen, Dick, Eileen and Russ with Louise and Ross

Sometime after Colin returned to Willoughby, Hugh and Laurel Frahn arrived and stayed in their self-contained caravan while Hugh built a shearer's kitchen. This was designed to share the existing kitchen chimney, and with a wall-hatch between the two kitchens to co-ordinate the cooking and facilitate communication. They left Adelaide to begin a trip around Australia but diverted to Evelyn Downs in response to an advertisement to work for Dick.

The shearer's cook, a big man originally from Denmark, who we called the 'Great Dane', added a bit of colour to the folk at the station. With the kitchens sharing an internal window hatch, the Great Dane and Helen struck up quite a friendship leaning over their respective benches by that window. While Hugh and Laurel were aware of a budding romance, Dick was oblivious to what was going on.

After the shearers moved into the men's quarters, where Colin had stayed, it wasn't long before evening darts started again.

A highlight for me at this time was the shearers burning warts off my hands, where more than 30 of the unsightly little blighters were growing. Warts were a very common affliction in those days and, fortunately, those blokes knew how to treat them. Their steps were to find a dry plant called buck bush, assess the size of the largest warts, break off a stem of that diameter and sear it to charcoal, then put about a centimetre of the charred bit upright on the largest wart and ignite it.

Because it was painful, they held my hands firmly and reassured me as it burned down, and then they flicked the stick off with the wart attached. After repeating the process on another two big warts, I had sore spots covered with Band-Aids for a few days, but with those big ones gone, the rest simply disappeared - and never returned. What an amazing cure, and all thanks to the shearers from who knows where. I have been forever grateful to them.

Hugh and Laurel extended their carpentry work after finishing the shearer's kitchen, and there was a lot of discussion between the Holts and Frahns that led to Dick's decision to lease them some of his land to set up their own small sheep station.

This was a very amicable arrangement, resulting in the Frahn's selecting a site for their homestead near the

Oodnadatta road, west of SM, on a rise near the boundary between Mt Willoughby and Evelyn Creek, which they called 'Copper Hills'. Fortunately, there was a lot of timber for building on the site and the country to the north was very rugged and colourful.

Laurel and Hugh at their chosen site

Dick helped them get started by using his plant to bore for water and Colin and I spent some weekends there to give them a hand. After they had completed their work on Evelyn, and the bore, windmill, pump and tank had been organised at Copper Hills, Hugh and Laurel moved there with their caravan and built a bough shed, but their plan was to build a rammed-earth homestead. Although that was a lot of work, the material costs were minimal and they could do all the work themselves.

They loved the bush and toiled unceasingly to make a future for themselves, starting by fencing their little property, which was very difficult in such dry, stony country. They had to dig all the postholes by hand, as there were no tractors with augers in that country, then string the wires and strain them by hand. In 2015, remnants of the original fences were still visible, with their original homestead set well back from the road.

When Dick took his truck into Oodnadatta to pick up loading, such as drums of petrol and other supplies, I sometimes went with him. Although the hotel served meals, we preferred eating at a boarding house dining room down the back street owned by Maisie Farley, a delightful Afghan lady who served delicious hot lunches to anyone who turned up. In the early days when Oodnadatta was the railhead, there were upwards of 250 Afghans living in and around the town who drove camel teams up and down the track to Alice Springs, taking loading to the cattle stations. After the rail extended to the Alice, and more hardy motor cars and trucks became available, camel teams became obsolete. John Kempe of Macumba Station, about 50km northeast of 'Oodna', purchased the last wagon team that an aboriginal man drove into town to pick up station loading.

On one trip to Oodnadatta we travelled at night with me standing on the running board, hanging out the doorway (there was no door), because it was so hot in the cabin. There was no air-conditioning in the 1950s! Dick made the cabin so that it would fit one passenger to the right of the driver, and three people to the left, but I'm not sure why. It was different!

The mail truck came once a fortnight and took three full days to complete its 1130km circuit when there were no mechanical problems or rain, all of it on bush tracks that went right past the scattered homesteads. Each trip was planned so that the mailman could deliver mail and loading and have meals and overnight stays along the way. Starting northwest of Oodnadatta on the Todmorden road, then west to Granite Downs, on the Stuart Highway to Welbourne Hill, Wintinna, Mt Willoughby, and then east to Copper Hills, SM, Evelyn Downs and Arckaringa, before completing the circuit back to Oodnadatta. If there was rain, the mail was delayed, until the road was passable, so there were never any perishables on the truck, even in winter. Butter was a rare exception because it came in tins in the days before eskies, but it wasn't very palatable and turned to oil in summer.

In my time, Jack Hanney was the regular mailman but Michael Tooth, heir to Tooth's Brewery in Sydney, drove it for a while in 1955. Borroloola Bob came after Mike and was quite a character. Dave and Helen Joseland of Everard Park Station were Mike's friends, hence his stint as mailman. Unfortunately, the mail truck shook to bits on the rough corrugated roads, so they chopped off the cabin with an axe and bolted the front together with Dexion. This exposed the mailman to the wind, rain, and sun, but he was always welcome at every homestead. When urgent mail had to be delivered to Oodnadatta, the mailman had to wait for it.

Mail truck at Mt Willoughby in 1955 with Mike Tooth

Stations ordered their groceries in bulk every six months or so from Adelaide and picked them up directly off the train in Oodnadatta by their own truck, but there always seemed to be extra loading to come out on the mail truck.

The boarding house, pub, and store were the only

businesses in the town before Jack and Ella Hanney built a new store on the rise towards the southern end of the main street. It was fresh, bright, and new - a treat and great addition for the town, especially its refrigerated items not available in the old store. Jack was a policeman in Oodnadatta and district before he and Ella decided to retire early and open the new store.

In later years, under new owners, Hanney's store has become the famed 'Pink Roadhouse'.

The AIM hostel was the first port of call for a 'cuppa' when station women visited town. The nursing sisters always made the ladies of the bush feel welcome, and occasionally visited their stations to get to know more about them and their isolated families. They provided a fantastic service, often in difficult circumstances, and were always busy looking after the medical and social needs of townspeople and travellers. Their two years of service also provided them with many wonderful experiences.

On one of my visits, the sister was bathing a tiny newborn aboriginal baby who had been born unexpectedly in the backyard dunny can. What an awful job to clean him up, but it had to be done, and the baby was none-the-worse for his unorthodox birth.

So, life in the outback was very interesting, with different things happening all the time, including visitors coming and going. Dick's mother was a dressmaker and while she was there, she altered some of my clothes to make them much cooler to wear, as well as making me a very stylish dress. It kept her occupied and made me happier. Others included a couple of back-packers who helped with stock work for a few days then moved on.

There was also a young couple, Bob and Daphne Ryan and their little baby, who lived at SM outstation and Bob travelled to work on Dick's motorbike. Daphne, a very young mother from Port Augusta, had a particularly lonely life with absolutely no means of communication, apart from the mail truck once a fortnight – not even a radio transceiver. Occasionally she and the baby came over with Bob for a day's company. Living in the bush makes people very independent and forces them to develop a variety of talents to cope with various situations.

Bob and Daphne at SM

When Mrs Brown at Mt Willoughby decided to buy some sheep, she ordered a truckload of rams from Adelaide that needed shearing. So Bob went to Willoughby to help Colin shear them, even though neither of them had done it before. However, they got the wool off and were very pleased with themselves. When Bob and Daphne left, another couple, Don and Margaret Davis with their two little children, replaced them.

One occasion when an acute feeling of isolation really struck me was when I received a letter telling me my cousin, David Grosvenor, a talented pianist who left Adelaide to work in Meekatharra, WA, had been killed in a road accident. It was a huge blow to my whole family and profoundly affected me, being very upset for quite a while, in spite of everyone's kind sympathy. That was when I felt isolation very deeply; when it wasn't possible to go home quickly to grieve with my family.

As I had cut my dad's hair for some years with old fashioned hand clippers, I got into the way of cutting the bushmen's hair, something that I have kept up to this day, although it is now much easier with electric clippers. Dick had a long comb-over (long hair on one side that was combed over the bald patch to the other side) which his mother encouraged me to cut off, but I wasn't game. Dick also displayed interesting talents with dentistry tools, and was much in demand for removing troublesome teeth. The early travelling padres also pulled teeth on many occasions, which avoided the pain, loss of time, and expense of getting the train to Alice Springs, Port Augusta or Adelaide for treatment.

Bob and Colin after shearing the rams

Dick bought a new car during winter that provided more comfort and status than the Rio ute, especially for the children who previously travelled in the ute's covered back. It was a Humber Super Snipe. Pretty flash. Its arrival was a great event. It had extra springs to give generous clearance for stony country and bush tracks. Dick was so proud of it - a new white Humber was so much classier than the more common Holdens and Fords!

Another fun occasion was when Bob and Rona Kempe at Mt Barry had a wine bottling and invited a few neighbours. We all went along and I became good friends with Bev, the housemaid/governess to Bob and Rona's three young daughters, Pauline, Erica and Robyn. When the 'adults' were getting merry with the wine, Bev and I turned off the lighting plant and all the men rushed out to find the problem, only to be thwarted by Bev who had it back on quick-smart and ducked out of the shed. They never did find out why it stopped - well, that's what we thought!

On occasional weekends, I went to Mt Willoughby and stayed overnight but Josie, the governess, was keen on Colin and therefore miffed when Colin and I took a shine to each other, but we enjoyed each other's company anyway.

One quiet evening Josie and I were in the kitchen having a yarn with the cook, Lou Manning, who was making a big batch of bread-dough; Lou was an inventive cook who dished up bright green mashed potatoes and other colourful food. After kneading the dough on the table, he patted it down then put it into a huge bowl, which he leaned over and made kissing noises.

We watched in awe but nearly wet ourselves laughing when he said that 'This bread has to rise to the lips of a great lover' because he was one of the ugliest old chaps we knew! He finished by wrapping it in a blanket, and then put it on the warming hob to prove overnight. Whatever else, he sure knew how to make bread because the fresh breakfast rolls the next morning were delicious - although I didn't enjoy them to the full because I was in love (with Colin) and had lost my appetite!

Oodnadatta folk

In September, we all went to Oodnadatta for the AIM-RFDS fund-raising celebrations where the Memorial Hall was set up for the various events, including a dance. The Reverend Fred MacKay, John Flynn's successor as Moderator of the Presbyterian Church, who we young women called Uncle Fred, always attended these events. He was a wonderful man, interested in everyone and everything, who was always keen to renew friendships with his station cobbers.

Because outback neighbours kept in touch with each other through daily radio 'skeds' (regular radio schedules), we knew each other's whereabouts and business, but the town folk were a different kettle of fish. However, I recall Reg and Sal Colby being very hospitable and good fun - Reg was a fettler who lived in a railway cottage.

Bill and Billie Lennon were also different, with Billie being very house-proud and seemingly always busy. As a former AIM sister with no children, we wondered why she was so busy, in spite of her spotless home. When Bill went out bush, he never returned home for a late lunch, preferring to eat his lunch out of town to avoid upsetting Billie, who didn't like serving late meals.

The Lloyds were also friendly and fond of beer and parties, but I wasn't experienced with the drinking scene and hated the thought of a hangover. In any case, I could never see the point - so I became known as a wowser.

New storeowners, Jarov and Jindra Pekanek were very hospitable and friendly and provided wonderful service for many years. When trains stopped at Oodnadatta to refill their water and disembark passengers and stores, the men jumped off and rushed to the pub while the women visited the store. They returned to the train when it was time to leave and the driver blew the whistle; men downing their last drinks often had to run to catch the moving train. What a sight!

Helen, nursing sisters, Louise and Ross at AIM hostel

Goods trains in the 1940s had a couple of flat-tops at the rear for aborigines to travel on, and when the slowly moving train passed through Oodnadatta, their townie 'cousins' ran alongside to catch up on the bush news. Such was the din, it seemed that they were talking and listening at the same time.

During this period, it was a time of great freedom for me with all my extra duties helping Dick, including trucking stores to Hugh and Laurel at Copper Hills, and my visits to Colin at Mt Willoughby.

When Helen wanted to go to Adelaide to prepare for Louise to enter the Wilderness Boarding School at North

Adelaide the following year, Dick wasn't too keen. But after she visited the nursing sisters and told them that she needed to see a doctor in Adelaide about a possible growth, she went later in the year. While she was in Adelaide Helen joined up with the Great Dane – she had a growth all right, she was pregnant with his child.

Ross stayed home with his father who, after he had overcome the shock of Helen leaving him, hired a succession of housekeepers until he married Meredith two or three years later, a widow with three children.

I was offered a housemaid position for 1956 with Mr and Mrs Scobie of Allandale Station, but as I was more interested in being a governess, I turned it down. Allandale was about 16km south of Oodna and Mr and Mrs Scobie were a quite elderly, dear couple, but I was for a more interesting life with younger people.

So ended an eventful year during which I had outfitted myself with more suitable bush clothes from RM Williams in Adelaide, as well as made-to-measure Cuban-heel riding boots and an Akubra hat. But I didn't have much cash to take home when Dick took me to Oodnadatta to catch the plane!

While I flew to Adelaide to regale family and friends with my tales of the bush, Colin rode south on his AJS motorbike and we met over the holidays and cemented our relationship. During that time, I met his Dad and Mum at Gilles Plains, and we spent a lot of time with his brother Ray and girlfriend Val who explored the Adelaide hills and beaches with us. We also spent time with both our families for Christmas and I caught up with close cousins who lived nearby when we were kids - our mothers were sisters and our fathers were brothers. As one of them was married and the other was 'going out' with a chap, we had lots of news to share.

In January, Colin sold his motorbike and bought a 1946 black Chev ute, which we used to go crabbing with his Dad, Mum, Ray and Val at St. Kilda Beach, a short distance north of Adelaide. This was another new experience! The water was very shallow for a long way out and we caught a bucket full of crabs, which we boiled and ate fresh. How delicious. Then we snuggled into swags on the beach for the night. What a great time after the conservative upbringing that I had!

At the end of the January holidays, it was hard saying goodbye to everyone, but my Dad and Mother were reconciled to me going away again because they could see how happy I was. Regrettably, I was going to be hundreds of kilometres from Colin in my new job and, with mail deliveries only once a fortnight, letters were going to be few and far between. I was taking a job at Delmore Downs in the Northern Territory, 240km northeast of Alice Springs, on a sheep station belonging to Dick's brother, Jeff Holt. My job was to supervise Jeff and Jessie's two eldest sons, Donald and Matthew.

A new adventure was to begin!

ALICE SPRINGS 1956
A Northern Territory experience

I arrived in Alice Springs after the long flight from Adelaide at the end of January 1956, to begin the school year – fortunately, the temperature was nowhere near as confronting compared to Oodnadatta. The aerodrome was south of Heavitree Gap, which provided the only access into the Alice for the Stuart Highway, the Ghan railway line, the usually dry Todd River, and power lines. The country was very dry and dusty, but nowhere near as barren looking as Oodnadatta. The Alice, surrounded by the spectacular MacDonnell Ranges, had plenty of trees.

Jeff Holt, Dick's brother, met me in Alice Springs then headed north on the Stuart Highway to just past the Tropic of Capricorn signpost, then turned north-east towards Delmore Downs Station, passing Yambah, Bushy Park, Alcoota, and through Delny. The country looked quite interesting and had a lot of bush, but was not stony.

My room was inside a spacious, comfortable house made of concrete and steel, which were common building materials in this area because timber was a feast for white ants. It had a single, screened door opening to the outside that made it quite private and two windows that made it very bright and allowed a breeze to flow through the door in hot weather. Thankfully, temperatures were not as high in the north, making life more comfortable, which was very, very different to the tiny lean-to at Evelyn Downs; it was furnished with two single beds, a wardrobe, and a dressing table.

There were lots of trees on the property, with a large gum-lined sandy creek, the Bundey, 50m west of the house. It was a lovely, very different situation compared to the barren stony plain of Evelyn Downs.

I met Jess, Jeff's wife, and their four children - Margaret the baby, with older brothers Richard who was three, Malcolm six, and Donald the eldest was eight. My job was to supervise Malcolm and Donald's school lessons in the breezeway, which was a new challenge. Fortunately, School of the Air was available from 'the Alice' and each boy had a half-hour session on the radio every morning. They were good, as much as boys can be, and had no trouble with their schoolwork. Their weekly lessons arrived/were posted on a Connair mail plane. This was a local service started in Alice Springs by Eddie Connellan, whose aircraft also did mercy medical flights. In those days, the flying doctors only worked out of Charleville in Queensland.

One Sunday later in the year when the young station hands were mucking about in their quarters, one of them picked up an 'unloaded' rifle and shot another one accidentally in the chest. We made an emergency radio call to Alice Springs and a Connair plane came to pick him up because it was too risky taking him into town by car. To get him there, he was loaded onto a mattress on the back of a truck and slowly driven to the bush airstrip where he was picked up and taken to hospital in Alice Springs; he made a good recovery but never returned.

Jeff did not believe that women should work with the animals, so I didn't get into the sheep yards like at Evelyn Downs and there were no horses because mustering was done by motorbike. Because of the very different work ethic, I went walking a lot, but only for short distances to avoid getting lost.

Jeff and Jess kept goats for milk that wandered freely in the house paddock, including a stinking billy goat, which meant that it was time to shut the windows when the mob wandered close to my bedroom.

Dingoes were a problem, but not as bad as wedge tail eagles that attacked and killed lambs and 'downed' ewes. For protection, Jeff put strychnine on a sheep carcase, resulting in a ring of dead eagles around it next day. Grazing properties enhanced the supply of water for their stock, which was also available for kangaroos, dingoes and eagles, enabling them to breed to large numbers that upset the natural ecology of the bush, although this wasn't noted as an issue in the 1950s. With higher stock-carrying capacity, properties in this area were smaller, compared to the Oodnadatta district, and they had fences that made them much easier to manage and control dingo numbers.

Jess employed a quiet, diligent, young, aboriginal lass, called Nora, to do basic housework, who came to Alice with us on our next trip because she couldn't be left alone on the property. However, she didn't return because she was pregnant.

Jeff's nearest neighbours were Alex Kerr and his wife Lottie who had migrated from Scotland to the mines in Broken Hill, where Alex worked as an engineer. Their little son was killed when a chimney collapsed on him, which devastated both of them. They came to the Northern Territory to take up a station called Delny, where they ran sheep. Alex started to build a concrete cottage, but he lacked the energy and drive to get beyond the most basic requirements. He followed the same path with his old Rover car, which had no brakes, so when he wanted to slow down for a gate or the house, he'd simply drop it into neutral and run it freewheeling in circles until it stopped.

They had another tragedy when a daughter was born at the station but died at only 15 months, which they never got over. More of the Kerr story is in *Beyond the Furthest Fences*, by Margaret Ford, and another anecdote of Alex in Chapter 9 of Kurt Johannsen's autobiography *Son of the Red Centre*. Lottie was a tiny lady who by 1956 was suffering with dementia and always 'going down the street to see mither' and getting lost. So Alex asked a friend, Mrs Agars, to stay and watch her and do the housework and cooking while he tended the sheep.

Jeff told us a story about a hot night when he visited Alec and Lottie on his way into Alice. Alec was starkers when he came to the door carrying a hurricane lantern and enquired 'Are there any women with you Jeff?' Fortunately, there were no women at that time.

Jeff loved going to Alice in his Ford Mainline ute and often took us with him for a couple of days, so we packed up, and with Jeff, Jess, baby Margaret and me on the front bench seat and the three boys in the back, we set off but stayed for a fortnight! On these occasions, Jeff always complained about the amount of luggage I took, but I got wise and packed plenty for any eventuality into my single suitcase. At that time Alice Springs was a small, interesting town where the oldest and most popular pub was the Stuart Arms, which was part-owned and run by Jessie's brother, Don Chalmers. I got to know Don and his wife Pam who lived on the east side of the town, over the causeway, which became cut off for a few days after rain when the Todd flowed.

Underdowns was another pub and a third, with only a floor and walls, was the picture theatre, with deck chairs and the aboriginal people sitting on the floor down the front. With no entertainment to speak of, people had to make their own fun. There was a club in town and occasionally a dance or live entertainment. I recall being invited to a dinner/dance with Don and Pam where I had a good time and met a lot of station folk.

There were always groups of natives sitting in the dry bed of the Todd River with such lively chattering. They always seemed happy. This was before the Government gave them pensions and the right to drink alcohol which caused fights when the wine (plonk) stirred them up, which resulted in them being banned from sitting in the river bed.

Wallis Fogarty's was the only general store, and there was a Chinese draper up the road and Heenan's milk bar. Wonder of wonders, the milk bar had air-conditioning - the first and only one that I recall in 1956 and they sold blissfully cold milk shakes. The Post Office was in the street fronting the railway line.

One day when I was in town, Peter Severin invited me to a race meeting and I donned a black shirt, buff trousers, and black flat shoes for the occasion. When Jeff saw me in

this outfit, he commented 'What do you think you look like?'
Well, OK according to me and no one else looked at me as
though I was from outer space! I think it was because Jeff
didn't like women in trousers!

Other memorable identities I met or knew about in town
included:

Miss Olive Pink who was born in Hobart, Tasmania, in
1884, worked for a time with Daisy Bates at Ooldea. She
was an eccentric known for her roles as an anthropologist,
activist, gardener and botanical illustrator, but I only knew
that she was different and didn't make friends easily. She
was the only person I ever saw in the bush who wore a hat
with strings around the brim that were attached to corks
that bobbed around to keep flies away. She died in 1975.

Chalmers Families. Margaret Ford wrote of the
pioneering family in *Beyond the Furthest Fences*, and Arthur
Groom mentioned them in his book: *I Saw a Strange Land*.

Mrs Lottie Chalmers, wife of Charles Chalmers
and Jessie Holt's mother, was where we stayed when we
were in town. She had a house in Bath Street where her
daughter Jean (Jess's older sister) cared for her and her
two children. Jean was a widow who owned Derry Station,
north of Delmore, and for most of the year, her children
were away in Adelaide at boarding school. We stayed in the
enclosed verandas; an additional seven people made it quite
a squeeze, but we fitted. We suspended lessons when Jeff
said we would only be away for a couple of days, but stayed
longer. The boys missed quite a bit of schooling during these
long stays, but they easily caught up.

Sometimes I stayed with **Pam Chalmers** over on the
East Side, who was very hospitable and we got on well
together. Don and Pam had a little daughter and owned
Dneiper Station, northeast of Alice Springs, but they didn't
live there; I believe that Mac Chalmers managed it. Don was

away from home a lot and was a part owner of the Stuart Arms Hotel.

Mr Charles (Grandad) Chalmers, pioneer

Charles (Grandad) Chalmers lived in the original stone homestead on MacDonald Downs, where he and his wife Lottie settled and brought up their four children, after a long trek across Queensland in horses and carts, shepherding a flock of sheep. Being very aware of indigenous skills, a large native camp near their homestead, they made the most of native labour in that lonely country. The natives showed a lot of love and respect for the Chalmers family and taught them about bush foods, tracking, and the local language.

In 1956, Mr Chalmers lived alone with only aborigines to watch over him, which they did with great respect and loyalty. The Chalmers' family also had a house in the Alice, which family members used whenever they were in the town. After Mr and Mrs Chalmers Senior died, along with the old natives, the mutual respect between whites and blacks diminished. The young people were a generation removed from the knowledge and care that their parents and grandparents received from the Chalmers family, and with the improvement in roads and transport, there was no necessity to keep the house in town, so they sold it.

The Mac Chalmers family also lived on MacDonald Downs, not far from the original homestead. Mac married Rose Agars and they had six children, the youngest Alex. In 1956, the girls, Heather and Annette, were away at boarding school, and Rose invited me to visit them in the holidays when the girls were home, to give them some company and me a break from the Holt children. Rose was an amazing woman – very musical. When they transported her piano to the bush on the back of a truck, she climbed up every evening to play it. She never used sheet music; she just played whatever came from her heart to her fingers. It was beautiful. She had natural talent.

Rose took great glee telling me about one of her sons, Jock, who was following her over a wide sandy creek bed one day and kept repeating the names of animals and birds whose tracks were in the sand – dingo, lizard, crow, cow, galah, old camel foot, lizard, dingo, cow, galah, old camel foot, etc. Rose turned around and said 'Jock, there are no camels here, so how can you see a camel track?' 'Oh mum', he said, 'old camel foot is you!'

A couple of times the girls and I walked with the native ladies to search for lizards and fat grubs under witchetty bushes, which they extracted with their digging sticks and immediately ate raw, minus the head. Ugh. Such enjoyment they had, working hard, laughing and chatting all the while. Mac, Don, Jean and Jess could all speak their language fluently, but I am not sure about the next generation.

Mac Chalmers was a huge, very strong, but gentle man who, it was said, could lift a 200-litre drum of petrol from the ground straight onto the back of a truck. Remembering the size of him, I could believe it, but many bushmen suffered a lot of back problems from their heavy work.

Rose was very kind and took we girls for picnics and to see interesting places in the Jeep, including a huge, perfectly round, deep crater called the Box Hill Meteorite Crater, which is now protected in a 474 hectare reserve named The Mac and Rose Chalmers Conservation Reserve. Rose kept in touch for a number of years and later visited my family at Glen Pedder, Greendale, in Victoria.

The McLeod family of Utopia Station moved there in the 1940s. Granny McLeod, who Colin knew but I didn't meet, was then a very elderly lady who had been blind since she was 12 years old. I heard that she grew up in Oodnadatta and later moved to Arckaringa station, which the family later sold to Mrs Brown of Mt Willoughby when they bought Utopia. Granny's grandson married the Delmore governess who I was replacing. Utopia was north-west of Delmore and the young couple paid us a very enjoyable visit when they were expecting their first child.

An excerpt from *Camel Train & Aeroplane, the story of Skipper Partridge,* by Arch Grant, relates a story about Mrs McLeod as follows:

The marvel of Arckaringa is Mrs McLeod. She has been blind since she was twelve. Folk say that three or four different men wanted her. This is to be believed, for she is a capital woman. Does all the work of the house, plays, sings, rides, trains the boys, and once when McLeod was absent for three weeks and the guide rope of the well tackling broke, she supervised and worked the whip for 300 cattle to water. Truly one of the 'women of the West' ... She reads widely, knows plays and players, speaks of seeing this actor or that actress, and is in fact the liveliest and best informed person on the place. She is very kind to Dick – he reads to her.

McLeod bought Arckaringa in 1914. There is a four-roomed homestead on the bank of Arckaringa Creek. He is just getting things into shape. He is a worker to the fingertips. From the tableland at the back of the house one gets a beautiful view away down the creek toward Nilpinna'.

Colin knew Granny McLeod and told me how she recognised any person she knew by the sound of their footsteps. She always greeted Colin by name, which amazed him, and would say, 'Hello, here's Colin and ... (whoever he was with) ... how are you?'

The Petriks of Mt Swan Although I didn't know them personally, they were well-known in the district and mentioned a lot. Mrs Petrik was Kurt Johannsen's sister and they lived over near Hartz Range garnet mines. The Holts had planned to go to the Hartz Range annual race meeting, but decided at the last minute that they'd give it a miss that year. Years later the Chalmers family bought Mt Swan and Charlie and his family now live there.

The Webb Brothers of Mt Riddock and other station folk. Some folk I met while we were staying in town at particular events; others I only knew over the transceiver from the RFDS base in Alice Springs. Years later, I met Bennett Webb during a stay at the Port Augusta Hotel run by Nan Nourse, when he asked me to supervise his son for a written examination in the home. As Station folk always stayed in the same accommodation, it was easy to make new acquaintances because people were pleased to spend time together. I also got to know **Sam and Daphne Calder** over the radio, who were from Argadargada Station, much further north-east on the Sandover Highway, but we never met personally.

Other folk who I met in Alice included Margaret and John Boyle, with whom I spent quite a bit of time when in town. They were English migrants, '£10 Poms', and loved Alice Springs where John was a warder at the gaol. Regrettably, we lost touch when I became very busy with the next phase of my life, and opportunities for visits were practically nil.

As well, erratic mail services in the Oodnadatta district did not help.

When we were in Alice, we always knew when **Dogger Allen** and his sons arrived in town. Normally they lived out bush where they earned a living by shooting dingos, for which the Government paid a generous bounty. Dingos were a huge nuisance to the station owners, decimating sheep flocks and cattle herds. Dogger drove a Land Rover with no canopy and with its windscreen down, with dozens of foul smelling dingo scalps (skin from the ears, down the back including the tail) hanging all around the vehicle. So you recognised them by smell as much as hearing and seeing them. Apparently, they made a good living and only stayed in town long enough to claim their scalp money and re-stock their provisions before going out bush again.

Kurt Johanssen moved cattle, mining loads, and general goods in his road trains. He was very well known as the person who introduced the movement of cattle by motor transport, instead of droving them to the railhead. Although the cost of trucking was high, much shorter travelling times meant that cattle retained their condition and could be loaded onto the train very soon after the muster. Droving on the road meant weeks where results varied according to the availability of feed on the way and gaining permission to pass through other stations, which were mostly fenced. With the cattle retaining their fat condition, higher prices in the market made it worthwhile. One of Kurt's road trains, 'Big Bertha', was retired to the Transport Hall of Fame in Alice Springs, where it is on display. He also transported huge loads of mining equipment, in which he had interests.

Opening of the John Flynn Memorial Church on 6th May 1956

This was a huge event but unfortunately, Skipper Partridge didn't come up from Arckaringa Station, even though he'd been a friend and contemporary of John Flynn for many years and contributed so much to his organisation, including setting up and maintaining the AIM hostels and transceivers. Skipper gave amazing service to the isolated, outback people for 40 years, but after he retired, he didn't go to the Alice any more. As we were in town, I attended the opening events, where I met a family from Katamatite in Victoria, whose daughter became a pen friend for a number of years before we eventually lost touch. The Prime Minister, Mr Bob Menzies, laid the foundation stone for the Flynn memorial two years earlier in June 1954.

John Flynn Memorial Church, Alice Springs

Jess was a member of **CWA of the Air, Alice Springs Branch**, when I joined and I still have a CWA recipe book published around that time. The recipes came from well-known station women whose names and stations were recorded. I affectionately remember the monthly CWA of the Air radio skeds when the district's ladies called in to discuss things of interest, including plans for a fund-raising event in Alice later that year. Because the CWA was such a well-known, respected organisation, I was thrilled to speak to so many women from within that enormous radius. I became familiar with their voices but never knew their faces, and they all endeavoured to be in Alice Springs once a year to meet together.

School of the Air, based in Alice was the same – once a year get-togethers in Alice to meet their teacher and the other children whose voices were familiar. Before the advent of radio-telephones and satellite communications, The Royal Flying Doctor Service transceivers were used for medical, social, and educational purposes and were an integral part of life in the bush. Towards the end of the year, Jess and I took the children to a school-of-the-air get together in the Alice, where they filmed the picnic meal. However, we were quite disgusted when the film company told the children to rush from the house, descend on the food outdoors, and then start gorging as though they hadn't eaten for a month. That was not how we taught them to behave, and many mothers were miffed at how they portrayed them.

Trip to Hermannsburg

Colin came and visited me at Delmore during the school holidays and we prepared to drive to Hermannsburg Mission to visit his brother Gilbert (Bert) and his wife Mona. Bert did contract maintenance work for the Mission; Mona (nee Kennedy) was a teacher at Hermannsburg, who came from the Barossa Valley. Bert and Mona had a toddler, Rodney, and a four-month old baby, Lance, and were happy to put us up for a few days. We stayed in one of the original, white-washed, stone married quarters that Kurt Johannsen's father built in the late 1800s.

When we were about to set out, there was an emergency call on the radio that we waited to hear – there was a tragedy in Alice Springs where Mrs Agar's son accidently ran over and killed his little boy, her grandson. Jess gave me the task of telling Mrs Agars at Delny, which was a very hard thing for a 20-year-old girl to tell a grandmother, but we drove across to tell her and comfort her in her shock. She immediately packed her belongings and we set out to take her to Alice Springs. Fortunately, we met Jeff and Jess on the way, with the three boys in the back of the ute, and transferred Mrs Agars to their faster vehicle. They had thought better of leaving the sad trip to us and decided to take the grieving grandmother into the Alice themselves. We were quite relieved, and drove through the Alice and out west to Hermannsburg.

We all fitted into Bert's Land Rover to travel to a place called Palm Paddock, a huge plain as far as the eye could see, broken up by massive monoliths of rock. As I recall, it was south of Palm Valley and the trip was incredibly slow and rough. I carried baby Lance in a wooden coolamon (a piece of curved strong bark to carry babies), which was much easier, cooler, and more comfortable than in ones' arms. On another day, we visited Glen Helen Gorge, which had wonderful rock formations of vertical strata and a waterhole at the northern end near the homestead.

Bert, Colin and I also visited Palm Valley in the Finke Gorge National Park, where rare cycad palms grow, and there is the Menengenenge Fertility Stone, which was sacred to the aboriginal women. It was there that they held all-women corroborees, when the women rubbed the stone to ensure healthy children and their own fertility. Although all the tracks were very rough and required four-wheel drives, they were wonderful days.

Colin with Rodney and Lance at Hermannsburg

Amongst his many skills, Bert was very clever at tanning kangaroo and euro skins, which an elderly black lady sewed together. Ray and Val, Colin and I, were later given beautiful skin rugs as wedding presents, which Bert said would be the only present he would ever give us. We used ours, called 'Desert Storm', on the bed for many years and it now hangs in the guest room in the Allendale house. A lasting gift, much appreciated. Ray and Val's was named 'Desert Star'.

On the road back to the Alice, Colin and I talked about getting married, and decided to get engaged in Alice Springs. I said I didn't need an engagement ring as they were expensive items and Colin didn't have much money, but he said every girl should have one and asked me what I'd like. I said I'd love a sapphire.

There wasn't a jewellery shop in Alice, but we were told that Mrs Jenkins, the opal buyer and gem collector, sold rings from her house. So we called on her and told her what I'd like and she showed us some rings. When we saw the prices, we decided that perhaps a sapphire was not the go; could she show us something a little less pricey. She then rounded on Colin and told him off - usually the man met her first to let her know what budget he had available and she only showed rings in that price range! So a sapphire was definitely out and we settled on a diamond. It was official, and we went back to Delmore where we were duly congratulated. I was only 20 years old.

When I celebrated my 21st birthday at Delmore my family sent a wonderful assortment of gifts, but they really missed giving me a birthday bash in Adelaide with my friends. I didn't mind! Jess gave me a table-cloth, but said it was neither for my birthday or engagement; it was simply a gift. I was a bit taken aback, but oh well Jess' way was different.

During the year when my cousin was flying from Adelaide to Darwin to visit her boyfriend, I happened to be in Alice when the aircraft had a scheduled stop and Geoff drove me to the airport to meet her. We had a lovely chat as there was much news to catch up on, including her relationship with Karl which was getting pretty serious, and my engagement and the date that we'd decided to get married.

The boys were pretty good with school, but three-year-old Richard was a bit of a terror. One day when I heard banging in the lounge, I walked in to see him bashing a nail into the polished wooden arm of the settee with a hammer. I was shocked and told him off, only to be roundly told-off by Jess, who said I had no business chastising him – even if he was wrecking the lounge room settee. Thoroughly chastened, I went to my room – ah – sanctuary!

Meanwhile, being a knitter ever since Mother taught me when I was a little girl, I knitted a little dress for Margaret, in which she looked quite sweet. She was a dear little baby and Jess was a very placid mother.

During the September school-holidays, Jeff's brother Dick arrived with his two children, Louise and young Ross, together with his housekeeper and her children. We had an interesting week before they drove back to Evelyn Downs. She was a lively bird, but their relationship didn't last.

So the year rolled on, with trips into the Alice to keep Jeff happy that bored the rest of us; I was glad to have other friends in the town. The peace was shattered when Mrs Kerr got lost in the bush on Delny after slipping away from Mrs Agars. With a frantic Mr Kerr, there was an anxious three-day search before they found her. Fortunately, the weather wasn't too hot and the aircraft were out, but Mac Chalmers ended up tracking her using skills that the aborigines taught him when he was a lad.

After that, Mrs Kerr left the bush and went into care in town because it caused too much worry having her on the station without a radio and only an old unregistered Rover car. Mrs Agars also returned to the Alice, leaving Alex to batch on his own and occasionally come over to Delmore for a bit of company.

Shearing started again when Harry Kunoth arrived with his children, including eldest daughter Rosie, who starred in the movie 'Jedda,' released in 1955; it was still doing the theatre rounds. Rosie was a quiet young girl who was born at Utopia like her father, and tagged along on his shearing jobs with the younger children. In the movie, she was called 'Gnarla Kunoth' and in 1960 she became a nun, but she left in 1970 to get married and later became an activist for indigenous people's rights. She now lives in Alice Springs or on Utopia Station. An amazing lady.

Jess hired a cook to run the kitchen during shearing, which only lasted a few days; everyone enjoyed the change of menu, Jess most of all. This time I didn't go near the shearing shed, much as I would have liked, because Jeff wouldn't allow it. Later that year there was a bit of excitement when a young station hand was accidently shot, as mentioned earlier.

By this time, I had heard from my parents about my engagement to Colin, and they were not happy. In their eyes, he was a beer-drinking, smoking, bushman. What sort of life would I have if I settled in the bush with someone like that? Colin's parents, who I met during the previous summer, were very happy with our match.

Not to be deterred, we loved each other and decided to get married in Adelaide on 26th January, 1957. Everyone wished us well when I left Delmore and when I went through Delny, Mr Kerr gave me a very generous cheque that he'd received. I cashed it in the Alice and, on Mother's advice, I spent it on a cutlery setting for nine people when I got to Adelaide – how much better than a setting for six when you have visitors.

During my short stop in the Alice I stayed in Bath Street with Mrs Chalmers until it was time for Jeff to drive me to the airport for my flight to Adelaide. I arrived in Adelaide in time for Christmas celebrations and the making of wedding plans. Colin drove down from Mt Willoughby and arrived in Adelaide about the same time as me.

When I was in Alice Springs, Dad and Mother bought a corner deli in Broadview, north-west of the city, and I stayed in a detached back room and planned to get married in the lounge room. Colin stayed with his parents. Although I had been a member of the Christadelphian Church, I was told that I was no longer welcome to attend services and that no-one from the church would marry us because Colin wasn't a member. Naturally, Dad and Mother were very disappointed, but I was determined to plot my own course and even more determined to marry Colin. Dad and Mother were very gracious in defeat.

PART II

THE CONTRACTOR'S WIFE

Mt Willoughby 1957 - 1959
Next

Mother arranged for our wedding to be at home with a formal reception in the city, besides sending out invitations. Meanwhile, Ray and Val had also become engaged so we four hardly remembered that Christmas.We were all busy with wedding plans!

Colin, Dianne and Miriam 26-1-57

My darling Mother had also purchased fabric and organised a dressmaker to make my wedding dress out of Chantilly lace and Miriam, my seven-year-old sister, was to be flower girl, also in lace. The dressmaker also made various other clothes for me, including my going-away outfit in navy blue Irish linen. Our fittings were done early in the new year.

Ray would be best man and fortunately, he and Colin already had good suits that they purchased for Gilbert's wedding, three years before.

Because of the church's attitude, my parents arranged for the Registrar to marry us in the house, with only direct family members present. Suited us! The last thing Colin wanted was a 'flash' wedding service – the reception would be bad enough for him, with about 100 guests, most of whom he didn't know. I assured him that they were dear people who I had known all my life, besides lots of my relatives. Colin and his parents only invited a small number of guests and there were only a few people from the bush.

Two weeks after we arrived in Adelaide, on 5th January, Ray and Val were married, with Colin and me in the wedding party. That meant that there was another dress to be fitted and sewn, plus a ceremony and wedding reception. Although Val's dad was an unknown quantity regarding his daughter marrying Ray, he relented and gave his daughter away, much to everyone's relief. Many of the guests were also Colin and Ray's friends who they had known since they were teenagers.

It was a lovely wedding and we were thrilled to be included, but what a busy time with two January weddings. Gilbert came from Alice Springs on his own for both weddings, with Ray as Colin's best man.

For my wedding, flower girl Miriam and I got ready at a friend's house a short distance from home, while Colin and Best Man Ray put on their suits at their parents' place. Colin thought he would choke wearing a tie, but as a concession, he rolled up his shirt sleeves under his coat! Although we had a civil ceremony, our reception at Balfour's in King

William Street was more conventional. Regrettably, some of my relatives didn't come because they disapproved of my marriage to Colin, which also hurt Dad and Mother but they did their best for their eldest daughter. Mrs Brown came from Mt Willoughby to attend the reception, where she reminisced about life in the 1920s with my Uncle Reg Spilsbury and his wife Clethra, who respectively had been a policeman and AIM nursing sister in Oodnadatta at that time. Clethra was Mother's sister and my Auntie! They had a wonderful time remembering former years, so I am glad that my Aunt and Uncle sat with Mrs Brown.

One couple from Oodnadatta who Colin had invited turned up but left quickly when they discovered that it was a 'dry' reception with no alcohol - they decided it was not for them. Don and Pam Chalmers also reneged, although they had accepted our invitation and were in town at the time - Pam dropped off an apology and a gift.

We received some lovely wedding gifts, including gifts that Skipper and Mrs Partridge delivered to the house on behalf of Mrs Brown, Dick and Mrs Lander, and Bill Fleming. It was all crystal pieces, which I treasure to this day. Thinking back, I wish we had invited the Partridges to the wedding reception to give Mrs Brown some company, but I was pretty ignorant and only sent invitations to people who Colin listed.

After the speeches were made and entertainment enjoyed, I changed into my lovely new outfit (which Colin subsequently told me he hated!) and we set off in the ute for the Adelaide Hills where we spent the first night of our life together at the Stirling Hotel. On the way through the hills, I had a sneaky cigarette and, without a thought, I threw the butt out the window. When we arrived at the hotel, thinking we were very suave, they took us to our room, whereupon mine host congratulated us and left us to it. During the night, we heard fire sirens that Colin always reckoned, from that day to this, were attending a bushfire that I started with that cigarette butt. He could very well have been right, as we discovered the danger of cigarette butts in later years when we lived in the extremely fire-prone area of Greendale, Victoria.

Next day we drove to Mt. Gambier where we stayed for a few days, with one day at the beach at Port MacDonnell where we went to separate bathing boxes to change for a swim. I got a shock when we ran down to the water and went in – my hero of a new husband had no teeth! He had left his false teeth with his clothes – horrors. I didn't want to own this gummy man, but agreed that it was very sensible to avoid losing them if they came out in the water.

On another day, we visited the Princess Margaret Rose Caves at Nelson that were discovered about 1930. When we visited as tourists in 1957, they were quite primitive, with Bunny Hutchesson guiding us through. The entrance was down some very steep wooden steps into the gloom at the bottom. Colin said later that he felt quite claustrophobic, but he didn't admit it at the time because he wanted to impress his new bride! Bunny was a very small man with a little pointed face and looked as though he spent his life burrowing in the earth, which he probably did!

We visited all of Mt Gambier's lakes where, being summer, the Blue Lake was very blue and Green's Lake was brown. We enjoyed seeing the Mt Gambier stone quarry, and the sink-holes in and around the area, besides enjoying the luxury of the nice hotel.

A week later we left Mt Gambier and drove into Victoria and up through the Grampians, passing a grass fire on the way to Stawell in the Central Highlands. That night we slept in the swag in the back of the ute and nearly froze because it was so cold. We got up early in the morning and, after looking around the Sister Rocks, drove north to Mildura and the warmth. We went to the Grande Hotel and asked for a room, and to our surprise, we were taken to a swish honeymoon suite. Wow, we thought, looking quite taken aback, until they realised we were not the couple it was booked for, and showed us to a tiny room down the end of a long corridor – much more suited to our pocket and there we stayed for a couple of days, sharing the bathroom with other guests on that floor. There were no en-suite rooms for our budget.

After enjoying a look around Mildura and a cruise on a paddle steamer, it was time to return to Adelaide, where we stayed in Dad and Mother's back room. Colin's Dad and Mum were upset because a Registrar had married us, not a minister, so they arranged for a Lutheran minister to come to their house and pronounce God's blessing over our marriage. We never told my parents as they would have been even more upset with us, but it made Colin's parents happy.

Mother later told me Dad had asked her, on our wedding night, whether she had a 'little talk with Dianne' about what to expect on the wedding night; but Mother said that girls knew everything in those days and she was sure that I would be OK. Thankfully I did, so I reassured her and she was relieved.

Now it was time to get down to the business of buying a caravan, to be paid-for and owned by Mrs Brown at Mt Willoughby. The plan was to take it back to the bush for Colin and me to live in wherever he was working, be it boring for water, erecting windmills, installing tanks, troughs, yards, and fencing, or stock work.

We chose a Furness caravan, and went to the Adelaide factory to buy it. It was about 4.75 m long and extremely well set out, but in 1957 there no refrigerators or gas stoves. It had a little two-burner spirit stove that was useless and quite uneconomic for bush living. We bought a small kerosene fridge that came in a wooden box, which Colin converted into a cupboard to hold the fridge. One side became a hinged door that protected it during transit on the back of the old red truck, but it stood in the annex under shelter when we camped.

Our only lighting was a Tilley pressure lamp, which shed an incredibly bright white light and warmth in the winter, but it added greatly to the heat inside the van on hot nights – and attracted moths by the thousands. The table had a folding leg that dropped between the seats to make the bed on which the back cushions were laid to become the mattress. It was very comfortable, but quite tedious to make up every night during winter. It also had a three-quarter bed with a single bunk above at the other end of the van that was handy to store things on. We mostly slept outside in the swag in warm weather.

My generous mother had given us loads of linen, towels and blankets, which I had saved in my glory box, which, together with our wedding gifts, made us pretty well equipped.

Northwards

When we were organised and had packed the ute and caravan, we hitched up and headed 320km up the highway to Port Augusta, where we left the bitumen. Being the end of February it was extremely hot going north over the next 800km of graded dirt road, the Stuart Highway, with its corrugations making it slow-going with the caravan. However, on our first overnight stay on the side of the road near Coondambo, a gorgeous sunset gave us encouragement for good weather.

We then took the road north-west from Port Augusta,

following the Adelaide/Perth railway line and past Pimba siding near Woomera township, which we bypassed because it was a government restricted area, to Kingoonya. From Kingoonya we turned north over horrendous corrugations to Coober Pedy, where we stopped to get petrol at Brewster's Store. The poor section of road carried most of the traffic to and from Coober Pedy to Adelaide and Port Augusta.

Brewster's store, together with Bert Wilson's Opal Store over the road, were the only two buildings above ground in Coober Pedy in 1957. From Coober Pedy we headed north over the cattle grid in the dingo fence and on to the 5,200km² Mt Willoughby cattle station. The road north of Coober Pedy was much improved.

A New Life

At Mt Willoughby there had been talk of converting the men's quarters, a two-room stone cottage, into married quarters for Colin and me. However, it was decided that the men needed their quarters and amenities more than we did, because we would be camping out on the station in the caravan most of the time. Whenever we took the van to the homestead, we parked it in the house yard and shared the only bathroom and toilet.

Dianne's Kitchen and Laundry

Every camp was set up the same as our first camp in the bush at Southern Cross Bore where Colin built a stockyard. After unloading the truck, Colin set up the annex, lit the fridge in the annex, and collected a good pile of wood to make a dense windbreak of branches about five metres in front of the caravan. Then he dug a damper hole with the camp oven beside it and lit a fire under a long steel plate mounted on short legs for me to stand my lovely new saucepans on. Next to that was a tucker box to store non-perishables, the bread dish, and a small stovetop oven to cook biscuits in. The washing machine and tub were set up at the other end of the windbreak.

At first I found it quite hard to cook on an open fire and bake bread in a camp oven - no-one told me that different wood produced different levels of heat (ironwood, desert oak, gidgee, mulga, dead finish, corkwood) – and anyway, how could I tell the logs apart? Sometimes the bread came out pale and soft, at other times it had a rock hard, black crust five mm thick, that I hurtled out for the birds. Once on a very windy day when I had wrapped the dish full of dough in a blanket and placed it near the fire to rise, the blanket caught fire, causing burn marks on the huge dish that lasted for many years. It was no easy matter scraping off the half-proved, burnt dough, before starting again - after feeling sorry for myself and having a good cry. I had seen bread made on the stations in huge stew-pans, so I followed suit, but I really didn't have much of a clue as to what I was doing.

Many years later, I realised that I should have been using a much smaller dish to mix the bread dough in, so bread-making quantities were experimental for a long time. The tinned Dribarm yeast had to be mixed with a little water, flour, and sugar then set aside to start 'working' in a warm place. That took half an hour or so, before mixing it into the bulk of sifted flour and salt with more warm water.

It was a guessing game involving digging the damper hole, filling it with hopefully good hot coals, putting the dough into the warm, greased, camp oven at the right time for it to rise again, then putting the oven onto the coals inside the hole with the lid on and coals placed around the outside and on the lid. Guessing the time required to cook the loaf was also a challenge, but I had some early successes, which was encouraging, notwithstanding the failures. Initially, doughy centres were a major problem, which I solved by placing an empty, greased, condensed milk can in the middle of the camp oven and laid the dough around it; the loaf cooked through and was much easier to slice!

The fact was that I didn't know much about cooking at all, so we ate a lot of steak when we had fresh meat; otherwise it was stew. The only 'fresh' vegetables were potatoes and onions – all others, like peas and beans, were tinned.

Dessert was nearly always tinned fruit, of which we had plenty, and custard made with Sunshine powdered milk – so easy to make. I later made steamed puddings and custard in the cool weather and they were very enjoyable.

Most of the meat was dry-salted and had to be soaked to rehydrate and reduce the salt content - another mystery to solve. Colin was quite helpful, but he'd only cooked on an open fire for men in stock camps where he also had his share of successes and failures – like the time he cooked rice and decided that a double handful for each person would be the go. Having started cooking it in the camp oven over the fire, he then added more water, then more water, until it was bubbling over the edges. That's when he found out that rice expands much more than he knew, and as a result they ate rice and more rice after that and the camp oven was a horror to clean.

We often had other men in the camp too, but cooking for a crowd was really beyond my experience. Fortunately, they were very patient with me as I dished up some quite unsuitable food for hungry men. The men simply threw their swags down on the ground when they arrived, then went off to help Colin before returning for tucker. Oh dear!

After all, I was a city girl with very little practical cooking experience. I had only ever cooked for my family of four and then only on a gas stove. Steamed pudding on Sundays and a cup of hot cocoa were about the limit of my experience!

The washing machine was very primitive – simply a drum on short legs with a perforated cone that was raised and lowered by a hand-operated lever. It was hard work! The water was heated on the fire and I used Rinso, a soap powder, to wash the clothes, but this was a major problem in hard water because it didn't make suds, just scum, which rose to the surface and had to be skimmed off. I wrung the wet clothes by hand before Colin screwed an old wringer onto the washer, which was a huge help. I rinsed in the big tub that doubled as a once-a-week bath. Normally I dried our clothes on an airer, or draped them over the windbreak; sometimes Colin erected a proper line with a wire strung between two trees, which was great.

Water was scarce - we were usually nowhere near a bore! Therefore when it happened, camping near a water hole was a treat.

Hand-operated washing machine. Courtesy of the Trigg family, Bungaree, Victoria

As Colin was a dirty worker in a dusty environment, I literally had to scrub his trousers and shirts by hand with a scrubbing brush on a hard surface. Consequently, his work clothes had a short life. Later, when Surf became the detergent of choice in the bush, there was a better chance for getting clothes clean with no scum, even with hard water. We all used Johnson's baby shampoo for our hair because it gave an excellent wash in bore water. Conditioner wasn't heard of until years later – but it also would possibly have gone scummy in bore water.

Sights to See

Sometimes we'd drive to an old well where there was no windmill and water was pumped into the stock tank with a diesel engine. They were interesting relics that sometimes still carried the huge steel buckets that a horse-drawn whip raised with a full bucket while lowering an empty one. The whip was a tripod of poles with chain and pulley wheels attached to enable a horse walking back and forth to haul the full buckets up and empty them into a trough. In 2015, we saw that the huge buckets had been retrieved and were on display at the homestead.

Another interesting place was Moonlight Creek where there was a monolith resembling Winston Churchill's profile that eventually eroded and collapsed. There was also a huge pile of horse dung nearby that Colin identified as a spot where brumby stallions offloaded their poo – always on the same pile!

I came to recognise some of the horses that came to drink at Southern Cross bore every afternoon, especially a heavy black horse with a big strong neck called Ajax.

After the worst of the summer heat, the autumn weather was warm and settled – very pleasant. Sunsets were glorious, spreading beautiful colours over the desert landscape.

When the yard and watering infrastructure were finished, we packed up and moved to Big Swamp to repeat the whole process, including a 200-litre water drum set on its side for drinking water. Colin put a bung (tap) in one end of it and dug a hole beneath the bung to make it was easier to fill the billy. A slight drip made the earth around the hole quite moist, attracting dozens of waxbills to the moisture. They are tiny birds and were everywhere, making a welcome addition to the quiet of the camp with their musical twittering. There were also huge flocks of budgies that settled on the surrounding trees, but they didn't come into the camp. Of course there were also the inevitable crows and galahs, and an occasional wedge-tailed eagle.

Colin didn't do much stock work when we were first married, being employed mainly on fencing the 65km² horse paddock, building yards, and installing a grid on the main road (Stuart Highway) to stop horses getting out when travellers came through.

Moonlight Creek monolith with Brad standing on top

Travellers were notorious for leaving gates open – not that there were many travellers in those days; only very brave people took on the dirt roads north of Port Augusta. However, there was quite a lot of traffic north and south to Coober Pedy, mostly miners, but not many travellers further north to Alice Springs.

In fact, it was quite an event to hear cars go by in those days on the Stuart Highway north of the dingo fence, which marked our southern boundary. There were usually only about four or five vehicles a day, notwithstanding it being called a Highway. It really was only a four-wheel drive track unsuitable for most city folk with sedan cars. Therefore, Land Rovers and trucks were the usual vehicles in the 1950s; by the 1960s, more people were getting adventurous, but many got into trouble on the road, either bogged in bulldust or mud if it rained, or damaged underneath by stones, or simply shaken to bits by the rough corrugations. Damaged sumps were common, followed by other big problems when the oil was gone.

Sometime after Colin built the cattle-grid, a load of mining equipment went through and broke the posts beside it and at every other cattle grid from Port Augusta to the Northern Territory. Naturally, there were many very unhappy station owners, especially those with fenced sheep stations south of the dingo fence.

To replace our posts, Colin scouted around for two of the largest trees he could find and cut very long strainer posts, which he then dropped two metres into the ground to prevent people moving them easily. The response was to try to push them over and when they didn't succeed, they simply cut the fence and drove through, with no attempt to fix the fences. They were very unpopular travellers, but Colin's incredibly strong strainer posts are probably there to this day as testimony to his good work.

Nights sleeping out bush were wonderful, the stars were so bright and moonlit nights were very special. Falling stars were another frequent pleasure, and it was so quiet you could 'hear' the silence and very occasionally a vehicle way off in the distance. Added to this bliss, the campfire was always a source of comfort and warmth. We often saw the Sputnik going over; Colin saw its first orbit in October 1957.

After only five weeks of marriage I became aware that I was pregnant - what misery feeling sick and with a vile taste in my mouth; we were still getting used to being married, let alone out in a camp with men around and everything else that went with camp life. With absolutely no privacy, everyone knew that I was sick and wondered what was wrong. I did not enlighten them. The smell of food became almost unbearable and I had no appetite at all; cooking was a trial. There was also no opportunity to indulge my whims and I got even thinner; in short, I did not enjoy my life at all during that time, except for the pleasure of using all of our lovely new things.

Colin also found it a challenge coping with a new wife who was sick and not very knowledgeable in camp. He had to provide me with a lavatory of sorts, initially with walls consisting of four steel droppers (star pickets) with an old oil-stained canvas wrapped around three sides (feet and head still showed), plus a 15-cm wide board lashed across to sit on, with a hole below. It was at least adequate, but it had to be a fair way from the camp – which meant that in a bare camp there was no mistaking when I 'went', often vomiting on the way. The joke about bush dunnies (lavatories/toilets!) was that because they were so far away, by the time a person got there it was either too late or they had forgotten what they went for!

Bath time once a week on Saturday involved setting up a 21 litre drum of water on the fire to heat, pouring it into the tub in the annex, then dipping into it with knees under your chin. Boy - was it cold in the winter, with the wind whistling under the caravan and flapping the canvas annex. Otherwise, we made do with a daily sponge in the caravan.

With water so scarce and mostly pretty hard, we managed on a 200-litre drum per week. I found the taste pretty awful and Colin went to the homestead and got a drum of good quality drinking water from the well for me.

When Colin's job involved boring for water and equipping the bore, he had a young fellow fresh from the city to assist him. Although he was quite young, he slept in a swag behind the firebreak. After a few weeks, his teeth turned green, so I reminded him that he should clean his teeth every day. I reckon he thought that because he was out bush and was saving water, he didn't have to worry about personal hygiene!

Bill, Brad and Colin shoeing Peugot

Once, between jobs, we went to the homestead and stayed in the caravan in the house yard for a while, with the young feller housed in the men's quarters. As I could not face any food at all, Reg Kyte the station cook at the time (Lou Manning had left), was very kind and sent me out a cup of tea and some toast every morning - but I couldn't face it. I had never liked tea and this was so strong that a knife could practically stand up in it. Adding to my misery, the 'toast' had been cooked under the lid of the Aga, making it a squashed, blackened slice of bread. Not what a pregnant woman fancied! Mashed potato was about all I could cope with because of the ever-present dreadful taste in my mouth; I also ate a lot of almonds that were in plentiful supply from a drum in the station store. Bland food was all I could tolerate.

Are you ready for a secret? Here 'tis...

One cold night Colin and I got fairly vigorous in the caravan after we went to bed, and rocked the van right off its stays. Woops. Colin had to get up and jack it up again – how embarrassing, especially with men sleeping on the other side of the firebreak! That was a night we never forgot! No one said a word in the morning!

Then ...

... we moved to a different job and my pregnancy began to show, so everyone knew why I'd been so sick and still was. In fact, the sickness didn't pass at three months, like I was told, and it never did until the baby was born.

Another problem I had with cooking over an open fire was that my skirts were not at all suitable. Because women's trousers were not common, but slacks were coming into vogue, many station women wore men's jeans. I sent away for a couple of pairs of women's slacks, but there was still a problem of how to cope with my expanding tummy - what could I do? I cut the front out, hemmed the raw edges, and attached tape to each side – problem solved! I had safe gear to wear in camp! However, there was another problem - we women always wore smocks as tops, which concealed my expanding tummy, but unfortunately they could hang over the fire and ignite. So I had to tuck them in when I was cooking.

After about five months, we thought it was time for me to have a medical check. With the closest doctor being in Alice Springs, we decided that I would go there to have the baby. So I planned to go north by train to have my check-up and stay for a couple of days at Queen Adelaide House, the AIM hostel for bush women, then catch the train back to Oodnadatta. There was no question of Colin taking me anywhere - women had to be pretty independent in the bush – probably still are.

Because Colin was so busy, we decided that I would drive the Chev ute into Oodna on the day the train went north, so I set out early and stopped at Copper Hills to say hello to Hugh and Laurel to see how they were progressing - Hugh had already started assembling the formwork for the rammed-earth walls. I then drove on to SM outstation to say hello to Don and Margaret Davis, who were about to take the children to Evelyn Downs to see Dick, Don's boss, so I didn't stay. About a mile beyond SM the muffler and exhaust dropped off the ute and dug into the dirt.

Shock, horror, I could neither drive forward nor reverse, and I had a train to catch with 130km to go. As I could still see members of the Davis family milling around the Reo outside their house, I yelled to them and began to run back. I ran and ran, and fortunately, they didn't drive off down the road to Evelyn before one of the children saw me. What a relief! The reason why they didn't leave immediately after me was because they had forgotten something and went back inside to look for it. God was looking after me that day.

Don drove me back to the ute and completely removed the muffle box and exhaust, threw them into the back, and I drove on with a deafening noise. Skipper and Mrs Partridge were not home at Arckaringa, the only other homestead on the track, so I continued non-stop until I arrived at Oodnadatta, by which time I was deaf and my ears were ringing. I left the car at Pattie and Bruce Evans' place, the local policeman, and he and his offsider, Bill Jacobs nicknamed 'The Camel', took me to the Ghan to go to the Alice. I felt very alone, and still deaf.

In Alice Springs, I walked to Queen Adelaide House in Todd Street, where I was welcomed and settled into my room, and in due course I saw the doctor. He found that I was quite healthy but he could do nothing about my all-day sickness. I arranged to have the baby in the Alice hospital and booked for me to stay at Queen Adelaide House around that time.

I then went to the hairdresser to have a perm, where I met Bert, Colin's brother, who walked in, sat down, and talked his head off. Bert and Mona, plus their boys had moved into the Alice from Hermannsburg and taken a block of land on Emily Gap Road, south-east of Heavitree Gap where they lived in a big shed. Bert had planted about an acre of lucerne to raise dairy cows and some date palms, following Vic de Fontenay's success with growing dates in the ideal Central Australian climate.

After all that, I was glad to get back on the train to return to Oodnadatta where Bruce and Pattie met me and had me stay with them for a few days because there had been rain and the road was impassable. That was an enjoyable break but eventually I had to go back to Mt Willoughby. Fortunately, the muffler and exhaust had been fixed in town during my absence, so I wasn't deaf when I arrived back at the station, which would have been awful.

Our next camp was at Box Hole, a lovely waterhole near the southern boundary of the station near the dingo fence. While we were there, the stock camp came through to do a muster in the area with all their camp gear and swags on packhorses. Seeing them loading the packhorses was a lot of fun as some horses objected to carrying packs and caused lots of ructions when they were being loaded up.

Rocky galloped around and tore through the camp gear, through a tipped out bag of weevilly flour that sprayed over everything.

When I was sitting on the yard fence, I thought that one of the horses was going to jump right over me, but at the last minute, he only veered past me. Phew, what a relief! I was taking photos – one of the few times we had film in the camera – but unfortunately, it all happened too fast to get a photograph.

Colin's next job was to build a yard at Doreen's Ponds, northeast of the homestead. He loaded up the truck and towed the caravan; I drove the Chev ute with the mechanical post-hole digger in the back. We called the digger 'Leaping Lena' because of its tendency to bounce all over the place in the back of the ute on its rubber tyres when we were driving over rough country, even though it was tied down. The digger was fairly new and made work much easier for Colin, who previously had to dig the postholes by hand using a crowbar and shovel.

As there wasn't a track into Doreen's Ponds, Colin pioneered one by walking ahead to check on the best way to go, and digging out some washaway gullies to get the vehicles through. Although it was only 18km from the homestead, it took us five and a half hours to get there, but we set up by nightfall. It was a lovely campsite with the ponds full of sweet water after recent rain – such a bonus. There were some wild ducks, so I took the rifle and shot one for the pot, which I plucked and cleaned before roasting it to make a delicious meal. It was a change from our monotonous diet of salt beef.

The crows really annoyed me at that camp, with their mournful carking as they sat in the trees on the lookout for scraps. I suppose I was a bit uptight with a miserable pregnancy when I got my rifle (only a peep site .22, but it was really accurate) and aimed for the crow - bang, I shot a galah out of the next tree! Well it was a bird and I got it, but I was quite mortified getting the wrong bird. In any case, it scared the crow off!

The day we went into the homestead after finishing that job, Mrs Brown and the manager were throwing a big party for wealthy Western Australian relations. They had a cook and a wonderful housekeeper, plus all sorts of other helpers. Although I was about six and a half months pregnant, we didn't mind joining in the fun, especially as it turned out to be the last of the prosperous years.

One of the less savoury results of many people staying at the station for a few weeks was that the septic system backed up. They had recently installed the latest up-to-date system, with a push button flush, but there was only one toilet and it wasn't designed for a large influx of people over an extended period. The toilet building was well away from the detached bathroom/store/laundry building, so it was quite a trek outside to 'go.' So, the station hands had the unenviable job of opening the tank and cleaning it out with shovels. Fortunately, that was the only time it happened, much to everyone's relief. As usual, the stockmen were great, having successfully met another new challenge.

*Mechanical post hole digger (Leaping
Lena) with ?, Colin and Reg Kyte*

The stockmen had their own 'long drop' closer to their
quarters, but well away from all buildings. It was a number
of years later when we moved to Gippsland in Victoria that
our children saw their first 'pull chain' lavatory, having never
seen such a primitive one before. They, like their parents,
hated the temperamental things.

As the time came closer for me to go to the Alice to have
the baby, my feet got colder, so I cancelled the bookings
in Alice Springs and arranged to stay with Dad and Mum in
Adelaide and leave the bush by the end of September, six
weeks before the due date.

We spent another short spell at the station homestead
where old Foosy was cooking, but as he used to get quite
cranky whenever I appeared in the kitchen, I tried to keep
out of his way. He made the most amazing, delicious rock
buns, though we definitely had to eat them the same day.
The next day they were indeed rocky and had to be dunked
in a hot cup of tea before they were soft enough to eat.

Eventually after Foosy left, the visitors had gone, and

the manager's wife was in Adelaide, the boss asked me to cook for the station - it was coming up to shearing time which would take only three or four days. But, when the shearers arrived he walked into the kitchen and told me to leave as he would do the cooking. Phew, that was abrupt, but I left him to it. When the shearers left, he walked out of the kitchen and told me I could do the cooking again. Apparently, I was useful when I cooked for the homestead and got paid for it, but I was very relieved when he went to Adelaide and left us to it.

Our next camp was on Arckaringa Station, on the road towards Oodnadatta, to put down a bore and equip it. It was the beginning of September, the weather had started to heat up, and hot north winds typical of springtime kept blowing out the wick in the kerosene fridge. I spent some miserable days trying to cope with this and the fact that nothing was very cool inside the fridge. Adding to our woes, the dust blew and because of the winter rain, the cattle had fresh herbage to eat that made their meat taste very 'weedy' and unpleasant to smell. But, as there was no alternative, even though I couldn't even bear the smell of the raw meat, let alone cook it, it had to be done because Colin and the men needed a good feed.

Fortunately, I left the camp on the 26th September and Colin drove me to Oodnadatta where I boarded the plane to Adelaide while he went back to camp. As it happened, Grandma Brown was on the same flight. When I arrived in Adelaide and was descending the aircraft's step (a DC3), onto the tarmac, my heel slipped and I fell down the last three steps. Fortunately, I wasn't hurt and not particularly concerned, but it seemed that all the airport staff saw it happen and rushed up, expecting me to have the baby on the spot! Naturally, Grandma Brown was also worried, but I was strong, albeit as thin as a stick because I still couldn't eat much. I must have looked pretty gaunt, because Mum cried when she saw me; I can now understand, since my daughter went through very similar pregnancies.

A couple of days after I arrived in Adelaide my cousin married her man after quite a long courtship. It was a very small wedding held at Uncle and Auntie's home, and of course, I attended. My cousin and I have always been very close. I enjoyed staying with Mother and Dad in Adelaide because they were excited about the coming grandchild – their first. Dad and I painted the detached back room to doll it up for me to stay in. The weather was warming up and very comfortable and I rode my old bicycle a lot to visit relatives in that area; Mum's customers reckoned that I would have the baby on the bicycle! There was an abundance of ice cream as Dad and Mother now ran a corner milk bar that also sold gifts, small goods, fruit and other items. I filled out with lots of fresh fruit, milk, and ice cream.

With baby nightgowns sewn, jackets, singlets and booties knitted, napkins bought and laundered, plus a little cane Moses basket for the car and a raised wooden bassinet that Mother used for Miriam when she was a baby, everything was set.

First baby, now two plus one

I enjoyed staying with Dad and Mother when mother worked in the shop during the day and Dad was the Stores Officer at the Adelaide Railway Station. He loved coming home in the evenings to serve in the shop and eat ice cream - he absolutely loved it and there was an endless supply, much to his joy and mine.

On my first visit to the family doctor, he was horrified at how thin I was, but said that I would fill out if I continued eating copious quantities of ice cream, fresh fruit and vegetables, and other 'normal' food during the following six weeks – which I did! By the time my baby was due I had reached my normal weight without a baby – so I was a lot healthier but still a stick woman with a tummy bump!

I booked into the Northern Community Hospital on the Main North Road, Prospect, where I was born 22 years ago. Closer to the due date, 5th November, I had my hair permed. But the pregnancy went past the due date and I got sick of waiting, so I took a small dose of caster oil one evening. Labour pains started about 5 am and I counted the contractions then woke Dad, who rushed me to hospital. He was thrilled, because he had a good excuse for speeding, although at that hour of the morning there wasn't much traffic. He wished for a policeman to pull him over so he could point to my condition to explain why he was speeding. There was no such excitement!

Well, I wish I'd had a bigger dose of that oil as the contractions faded away and the staff had me walking up and down the corridors to try and bring on this baby. Eventually it arrived - a gorgeous little girl - 24 hours after I arrived at the hospital. She weighed 7 lb. 13 ozs. and had peaches and cream complexion and a lovely covering of auburn hair. It was November 10th and we named her Del Elizabeth. Every detail was perfect and the staff showed her off to everyone who came along.

A friend of mine, Barbara, had a baby boy an hour before me on the same morning, who they named Stephen. I'm glad I had a girl, because Steven was the name we'd chosen for a boy.

Dad and Mother were my first visitors and only family members were allowed to visit during the first five days, the length of time that the new mums were kept in bed 'to regain their strength' and be supervised when 'the milk came in' at about the third day. I stayed for ten days because I was so thin; Mother cried again when she saw my skinny legs.

Dad and Mother sent a telegram to Colin, who had said that he wouldn't come to Adelaide when the baby was born. However, when his boss sent someone out to the camp to let him know he had a daughter, he finished the job he was doing and drove non-stop for 24 hours to Adelaide, where he turned up at his parents' house, told them the news, had a shower, and arrived at the hospital about 9 pm. The staff regarded him as a great hero for coming all that way and because Adelaide people had a great love and respect for bush people. Colin was allowed to visit me and nurse the baby, even though it was strictly against the rules for husbands to come after visiting hours. We were very spoilt.

Needless to say, I could not stop telling him about the whole experience, which he patiently listened to, over and over again and he could not stop grinning. When visiting hours were relaxed, many relatives and friends came and spoiled us with gifts for our baby girl.

Like all new mums, I was encouraged to drink lots of water, which had to be tank water because I could not tolerate the taste of Adelaide water. As a result, the extra fluid made my breasts so engorged that the staff pumped about 250ml from each breast to relieve them. Cracked nipples didn't help and were made worse by a baby with a strong suck, and the nipple cream that we were advised to use was completely useless. So there I was thin as a stick, having exchanged tummy bump for breast bump. Fortunately, by the time I was ready to go home Del Elizabeth was putting on weight, my breasts had started to decrease in size, and the nipple soreness was almost manageable.

Meanwhile, my brother David who by then was married, flew in from Sydney, looked at my baby, and could not believe how lovely she was. How could his sister produce that? He thought all babies were red, wrinkled and ugly. Ten months later when David and his wife had their first child, Martin, he was red, wrinkled and ugly at birth and David was devastated. It took him a couple of days to realise that a baby's appearance changes rapidly after birth, which was the case when Martin filled out and developed into a little cutie.

All of Mum's customers wanted to see the new baby because she certainly was very cute and happy – until about 7 pm when she started crying and nothing could stop her, nothing, until I fed her about 9.30 pm, and put her to bed where she slept until her early morning feed. In those days, we were instructed to only feed our babies every four hours (definitely not on demand), and that crying had to be tolerated if baby was fed, 'comfortable', and dry.

Colin and I were happy to be together again after my six-week's absence and thoroughly enjoyed showing our new baby to everyone. We celebrated Christmas, 1957, in Adelaide with both our families and as Colin wasn't needed back at the station for a while, we spent most of the summer in Adelaide, staying at Broadview, which was very comfortable.

Gilbert and Mona, and their boys were also in Adelaide for a holiday, staying with his parents, and we asked him to make a collapsible, mobile, meat-safe cot for Del, like the beauty he made for his boys. Unfortunately, instead of doing the work in Adelaide he decided to tackle it in Alice Springs where he got tradesmen to do most of the work, who charged the earth for it. The cot ended up costing about £100, which was a huge amount in those days when Colin earned about £20 a week. But, it was a great cot when we picked it up later in the year.

While we were rejoicing in Adelaide, the notorious Sundown murders happened on the side of the road near Kulgera on the abandoned Sundown Station, well north of Mt

Willoughby. Bruce Evans was the attending policeman, and Jack Hanney, a former Oodnadatta policeman, was called in because of his expertise and local knowledge. He later showed us a movie of when the bodies were uncovered – a very grizzly sight that reinforced our empathy for the police because of what they sometimes have to deal with.

[Google: 'Sundown Murders' for information of this awful event; also 'Jack Hanney, Oodnadatta', which directs you to *Blast from the Past, Reminiscences of Charles Hopkins*, on the SA Police Association Historical Society Newsletter site, Nov 2009.]

At the end of January 1958, we set out for the station once more, with the baby in the carry basket behind the seat of the ute, or in the basket between us. Although it was pretty hot, we managed well, as did our baby, and it was much easier travelling without a caravan.

Back at the station, everyone admired Del and we settled back into the caravan. Because the weather was still hot, Colin and I slept outside the van and we took out the single bunk from above the three-quarter bed and put the basket and later the cot when it arrived on the bed. I enjoyed our little baby but Colin was a bit funny with her – he didn't quite know how to hold her. The men were the same, with Bill Fleming in particular looking quite awkward as he held her out in front of himself – because he was afraid that she would leak out of her nappy, not realising that she had plastic pants to keep the wet inside!

Each month I received a letter from the Mothers & Babies in Adelaide to inform me of the average progress of babies, and Del was pretty well normal in her growth, which was quite reassuring for this new mum. I took her into Oodnadatta for her vaccinations when a doctor from Port Augusta visited.

At race time in April, I was pregnant and sick again and

most of the station family and staff went into Oodnadatta early to clean the Mt Willoughby shack. Colin and I stayed back at the station to go in later, and Mrs Lander asked me to cook a batch of fresh bread for the crew in the town. I baked the bread in the Aga cooker then, probably because of the work and strain, I miscarried. It was very early in the pregnancy – only a few weeks, but I kept going. Although I felt awful, there was no one to turn to for help or to carry some of the work-load, but at least I didn't feel sick anymore. We then drove into town, taking Colin's off-sider with us, and stayed at the Mt Willoughby shack with our swags thrown down on the north side veranda.

I had mentioned to Colin that it would be nice to have a bottle of champagne at race time to celebrate our baby, but he reckoned champagne was too expensive for the likes of us.

Anyway, after the Monday races, the actual cup was filled with bubbly and passed around for everyone to have a taste. We all had a good time. Tuesday morning Colin wanted to leave town before lunch, so I packed and waited for him to come. His off-sider, who was not a party boy, was ready anytime we were, but Colin did not come, and did not come! I was getting a bit browned off, so I slowly drove down the street past the hotel and there he was – upending a champagne bottle and gasbagging like you wouldn't believe with Rusty Coombes, another contractor in the district. It was quite a while before he returned to the shack, decidedly worse for wear.

Mt Willoughby Shack

We eventually set out with Colin driving, but after about 10km, he declared that I should drive, with Del behind us in the basket. The truth was that he was feeling decidedly unwell and wanted to go to sleep, so I drove home while the others all slept. And I never did get my bottle of champagne!

I suffered from ongoing extreme hay fever in the bush, aggravated by the dust. In those days, the only relief was anti-histamine tablets called Avil, which I used constantly to try and control the sneezing and runny nose and eyes but I was always uncomfortable and went through hundreds of tissues which were kinder on the nose than handkerchiefs.

Non-stop sneezing is extremely tiring - once I counted 36 sneezes without stopping, which left me exhausted. Some days the hay fever developed into asthma and I had trouble breathing, so I went about feeling groggy much of the time. Fortunately, one of my cousins was a pharmacist who was able to supply enough tablets to keep me going. A dusty house in a dusty climate didn't help.

Our next camp was at Pooramingie Bore where Colin put a bore down before we were married, and was now equipping it with windmill, tank and trough, having already erected the holding yard with a bronco peg for branding calves. Sometimes he had men helping him if they weren't mustering or doing other station work.

Pooramingie mill, tank & trough–all Colin's work.

Del was sitting up by this time and was a good baby, crawling around the caravan floor every day after I washed it, playing outside on the rug that I laid over canvas, or in her meat-safe cot where she was quite safe and protected from the flies. Fortunately, as it was winter, the flies weren't a bother at that camp.

When the men were called away to another job, I helped Colin with the mill. He had already erected the tower plus a gin-pole and pulleys to raise the head onto the 16 m tower. With pulleys attached, he reversed the truck to raise the head, which weighed about a tonne, above the level of the top of the tower. He then put the brake on, got out, and climbed to the top of the tower, while I drove the truck inch by inch to lower the head into position with Colin hanging on the top by his legs and arms, watching the head come down towards him. I sweated over that; one jerky move and the whole thing could knock him off his perch and it would have been 'goodbye Colin.' I felt a great sense of achievement when we completed it safely.

Needless to say, Colin was also pleased with my driving and the fact that we had accomplished a difficult, tricky job together. The mill had a 7.5m diameter wheel which he had assembled himself - the largest in the district at that time.

Not long after, a big wind bent the tail back onto the wheel and experts came from Adelaide to inspect it. Initially they blamed Colin for not assembling it correctly, but they revised that when they found that the holding joint was simply not strong enough, and they replaced it.

One weekend we went to Everard Park for a celebration with a big crowd of neighbours; it was always good to get together. We all took our swags to stay the weekend and Dave and Helen Joseland were very hospitable. It was a wonderful party.

Dave and Helen were good neighbours, although we rarely saw them. In younger days Helen played the role of the youngest daughter in the 'The Overlanders' movie with Chips Rafferty. Some of us drove out to the Everard Range on the property, where there was a bright green patch in one of the gullies, a permanent spring. The yards were very solid because they were from larger mulga trees than we had at Willoughby although, as always, the posts were crooked. Mulga is a rugged, though not tall, tree with hard wood that was good for yards and fence posts.

After returning home, we went to Corkwoods swamp (dry) where Colin started to drill for water in the middle of the swamp, but it rained and rained for three days and nights, 76 mm, which was wonderful when our average annual rainfall was only 100 mm. However, Colin couldn't work when the swamp filled with water, and by then his offsider had moved on, leaving only Colin, myself and baby Del in the wet camp.

It wasn't easy living in a tiny van with nowhere to go and nothing to do except play and look after Del when she was awake. I couldn't even cook because it was too wet outside for a fire and the spirit stove could basically only heat enough water for cups of tea and Del's daily bath, which I then used to wash her nappies, before rinsing them in fresh water. Coffee came in bottles labelled 'Coffee & Chicory', or as grounds to boil up. However, there was a bright side - it was the only camp with a decent loo, which Colin made with posts, wire, and brush – it was a doozy. I wish I had a photo of it.

As soon as the rain stopped and the country began to dry out, I lit the fire outside to make bread. When I dug the damper hole I cut a little frog in half - and didn't I cry – but too late – it was already dead! I managed to build up enough coals to cook bread, which was a great relief after our wet camp. I also dried Del's napkins.

As we didn't have a transceiver in our camp, we were cut off from the world, but we had our battery-operated mantel wireless, which we tuned to listen to the shortwave RFDS radio. Before the battery died, we managed to hear a distressing message about a tragedy in the district, but had no idea what it was. On those occasions we felt extremely isolated, being about 48km from the homestead and unable to drive out in the old truck and without a four-wheel-drive vehicle.

A few days later we heard a vehicle, which turned out to be the station's Land Rover driven by Brad Russell; he had come to see if we were OK and check if we had enough food. He told us that Don and Margaret Davis' little lad, Johnny, drowned in a waterhole in Evelyn Creek just below SM. The boy went for a walk with his sister while their mother Margaret was having an afternoon rest, and they were playing in the water when Johnny couldn't get out. By the time the little girl ran back to the house and said to her mother (who was about eight months pregnant), 'Mummy!,

Mummy!, Johnny won't come out of the water', it was far too late.

Johnny's grave on the rise above SM, photographed in 2015.

The news went out by radio and in spite of great difficulty on the boggy roads, Skipper Partridge from Arckaringa, together with Bob Kemp from Mt Barry and Dick Holt from Evelyn, got through together, made a little wooden coffin, and buried Johnny on the hill overlooking SM. Sadly, the police couldn't get there in time and the whole district was shocked, but because Skipper was a minister, people thought that Johnny was buried well. After that, Don and Margaret left Evelyn and no one lived at SM again.

When Del was about 10 months-old she was walking around the caravan hanging onto the furniture, but she stopped when we moved temporarily into the homestead after the family went south and I was doing the station cooking. The house was a big scary place for a tiny girl to walk around after the security of the small caravan and it was another month before she resumed walking alone. Then she got gastro-enteritis, which was dreaded in the bush. However, when I contacted the doctor at Port Augusta via the medical sked, he prescribed sulpha drugs from the comprehensive RFDS medical chest where all the medicines were numbered and ready for use. Fortunately, she was very good at taking her huge tablet and soon recovered.

About this time the manager's brother, Mack, together with his wife Myrtie and young children, took up some land west of Mt Willoughby on a block they called 'Blue Bonnet.' Because it was dry out there and they lived in a couple of caravans, they came into the station for water and supplies. Myrtie was a wonderful cook who could even make sponges in the camp oven, as well as being an experienced bush woman – very different from me. They were there only a couple of years before deciding that it would be too hard to stay, so they moved on, with Myrtie and the children going to Alice Springs where the children could be educated.

Blue Bonnet had a change of name later and became Cadney Park, not such a pretty name (cadneys are lizards). It is now a well-known stop on the Stuart Highway, north of Coober Pedy but before Marla, a township on the highway that was then simply a mill, tank, trough and yard. Mt Willoughby Station is now east of Cadney Park and bypassed by the highway.

*Oodnadatta main street as it was. Photograph
by John Armstrong, with permission*

Colin cutting a fence post with his first chain saw

Rose and Mac Chalmers in later years

Dianne rubbing the Menengenge Stone

Coondambo sunset

On the move 1957

*Rocky didn't want his load. Pack ready to go on
(right) Swag in the right foreground to be loaded*

*Our new cottage, unfinished, with ute on the left and
three generations of women, including my sister on the
veranda, and my parents' caravan on the right.*

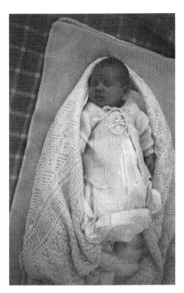

*Our baby daughter Del,
three weeks old*

Dianne and Del in the rough

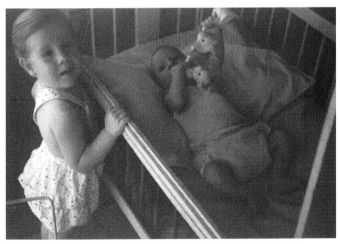

Happy children

Helen and Del at the station horse-breaking yards

Brad giving us some excitement

Colin breaking in Redbird

Del and Steven in the shed watching the dust

*Bus people–driver on left, then Helen, three ladies,
Jack Hanney, Dianne, two ladies, Del and
Steven in front with the dog*

Bill on the bronco horse pulling up a calf

Colin riding a calf

Cutting out at Arckaringa

Cessna coming into land on station airstrip

Children at Branson's Rockhole (spot Steven)

Di, Colin and Del 1958

Once again, I was pregnant and once again, I felt really dreadful. I weaned Del at 11 months after she twice bit my nipple (excruciating!), so that was that. She was a dainty little tot who toddled about 'talking' to everyone and could walk right under the kitchen table without ducking or bumping her head, where she patted the men's knees. They thought she was cute.

Bert and Mona, and their two little boys Rodney and Lance, called through on their way down to Adelaide for a break and stayed for a couple of days.

Unfortunately, because I had the place to look after, plus cooking and looking after my own family, I didn't have a lot of time to talk to them, but Mona was on holiday and rested.

We went to Adelaide for Christmas and some of the

summer but it was very different travelling with a baby. We camped on the side of the road somewhere past The Twins station on a hot, bright moonlight night and put our 13-months old Del down to sleep in her folding meat-safe cot, but she didn't settle even though she was so tired. So we had the brilliant idea of knocking her out with a bit of brandy in her bottle of milk. Well, by the time I came to measure some out I got chicken and only put in a little bit, which had the opposite effect and really woke her up. She was up and down the cot like a caged lion, talking to us and to the moon, until we gave up trying to sleep and packed up, and moved on.

In Adelaide, we stayed with Colin's parents at Gilles Plains, along with Gilbert and Mona. While Mona worked at setting up a crossword, and she kept to herself, Nana and I did the meals, the housework and looked after the children.

Dad and Mother had sold the shop and until they decided where they wanted to live, they stayed at Warradale with David, Marion and baby Martin.

Another summer passed and we went back to the station to spend another year, much as usual. With our second baby due in June, the thought of living in the caravan with two babies was not my idea of an ideal life, so Colin gave notice and was 'snapped up' by Ian Rankin to work as a boring contractor at Mabel Creek, a sheep and cattle station 130km south and below the dingo fence. So we packed our few things onto the ute and left Mt Willoughby for Mabel Creek, not long before the baby was due.

MABEL CREEK 1959-1960
2nd baby

After we settled into the huge shearers' quarters at Mabel Creek Station, Del and I flew to Adelaide to wait for the new baby, due in a few weeks. As I hadn't seen a doctor since getting pregnant, I visited a doctor in Adelaide who said everything seemed to be going well, apart from me feeling sick all the time.

As we didn't want to be away long, we stayed with David and Marion and their baby Martin, together with Dad, Mother and Miriam. It was a bit of a squash but we managed. It was fun being together.

Once again, Dad did the honours with the car in the early morning hours before Steve was born at the Northern Community Hospital late in the afternoon. Some of the same staff were still there, who welcomed me with open arms, and again I was kept in bed because I was so thin, but I soon picked up with all the good food. However, I didn't attack the water jug so much and my breasts were much easier to manage. Steven was a good baby.

This time Colin didn't come to Adelaide; he decided to stay on his new job at Mabel Creek sheep station where there were a lot of staff and he was boring for water as Ian (his boss) was setting up new paddocks with a fencing contractor who had his own family camp in the bush.

All went well with Steven's birth but he wasn't as beautiful as baby Del, causing some to comment: 'Oh well, his mother would love him!' In fact he looked just like Charlie Kunoth, a neighbour on Mt Clarence Station, east of Mabel Creek, who was no oil painting!

Where Del had been a dainty little girl, Steve had long arms and legs and barely fitted into the little carry basket that Del had used for a couple of months before she outgrew it. Before Del's birth, mother had knitted some gorgeous little jackets in which Del look so sweet. She did the same for this new baby, but it was quite a different story - the jacket's arms only reached down to Steve's elbows and he had almost outgrown them before he wore them. There had to be some fast knitting for this winter baby!

Mother was wonderful whenever we went to Adelaide, ringing up my friends and taking me visiting - everyone was captivated by my tales of the bush and my dear little, red-haired girl. Del was able to wear some of the lovely smocked dresses given to her when she was born, but which she had no opportunity to wear in the bush.

When we visited a particular friend in a flat in Salisbury, north of Adelaide, she had a lovely time with Del before taking her outside to play. Then, oh my goodness, Del fell onto her just-watered garden and muddied her clothes. So we took her back inside where we bathed her, then 'dressed' her in one of her husband's singlets. Fortunately the weather was warm, but what a funny sight! Oh well, life is full of such little events! I didn't think of taking a change of clothes for Del and she had never seen a garden being watered!

In those times, it was usual to ask little children what they could say before they could actually talk, such as: what does the puppy dog say? - 'bark bark', what does the pussy cat say? - 'meow,' etc., but when they asked her what does the birdy say?, she responded with a loud 'cark cark', much to their shock, then amusement. My little girl had only heard galahs and crows, more crows than galahs, but she knew they were birds and that was what birds said. No dainty tweet tweets for my Del!

Some weeks later Del, Steve and I were back in the air returning to Oodnadatta. Colin was there to pick us up and take us back to the quarters to settle in, but it was a much longer drive this time, calling at Arckaringa, Copper Hills, Mt Willoughby and the homestead at Mabel Creek to show off our new baby boy. At the quarters, 16km from the homestead, Colin and I used the cook's bedroom with its adjoining shower room (sounds flash, but it wasn't – poured concrete, no paint, and no inner door). The children had separate bedrooms along the veranda, with Steve in the meat-safe cot because he was too big for the little basket, and Del in a new wooden cot.

Ian Rankin secured a milking cow for us, which was great, although she was cunning and used to hide behind trees when I went looking for her in the afternoon. However, it was wonderful to have fresh cold milk to drink from the fridge - and the clotted cream. Delicious! The kerosene fridge, an old-fashioned one on legs that belonged in the quarters' kitchen, was wonderfully efficient.

With so much milk and Colin away working, I decided to take the children for a drive to deliver some milk to the fencing camp, which I knew had small children. It was a bit of a gamble, but I roughly knew where they were fencing and the country was flat, lightly timbered, and easy to drive over in the ute. So off I set with Steve squashed in the carry basket behind the seat and Del in a little toddler seat clipped over the back of the bench seat. The toddler seat was basic in the extreme and if the little one went to sleep, we put a little pillow under baby's head to prop it up.

Now I had to find the fencing camp! Eventually I stopped the ute and got out to listen for the men working. I then drove towards the noise and found the camp where the fencer's wife was glad to see another woman for a yarn, especially one with a flagon of fresh cold milk in her hand. They had an older child and a little toddler, who was playing in a 'tea-chest' – like the one that I packed my good crystal in straw to travel the country on the back of the truck. It was quite a novelty to see this little one standing securely in the tea chest, happily playing. I have found that when children can see a parent they are usually quite happy, but when the adults are out of sight they start fretting. We had an enjoyable visit, which unfortunately was not repeated because they moved to another campsite further away.

Steven was a good baby who I only breast-fed for about four months, but he made good progress with his weight according to the monthly progress charts that I got from the Baby Welfare HQ in Adelaide.

Water fountain on stove. The Mabel Creek stove firebox extended the whole width of the top with the two ovens side-by-side beneath. Courtesy the Trigg Family Bungaree, Victoria

The children kept me busy when we were alone in the shearer's quarters, which had many bedrooms off the verandas and a massive dining room with lots of long trestle tables with forms to sit on. It also had an open kitchen with a range about two metres long and 75 cm deep, suitable for cooking for a big shearing team. I only used one side of the huge firebox, but it heated a huge cast-iron water fountain with a side-tap that sat on top of the stove. Cooking bread and roasting meat in one of the side-by-side ovens was a pleasure after the open fire and the camp oven, which I never used again.

Hot water for showers and the laundry came from a wood-fired donk (boiler) at the other end of the building, but the water was very hard – requiring hard work with the hand washer and more scrubbing of Colin's clothes.

When I was in Adelaide, I bought a small, new-fangled, transistor radio with a moveable solid aerial, which I made to work by wrapping a length of soft wire around the aerial. It then picked up the signal from Adelaide's commercial radio station, 5CL, over 1,000 km away, which gave me a real treat listening to the morning variety program featuring news, music, and a quiz. The trick was to guess different sounds, for which there were two prizes, one for the most distant listener and the other with the correct answer. I knew instantly that the first prize was mine and sent off an entry by the next mail. Sure enough, in due course they announced my name as the most distant listener with the correct answer. What a thrill.

The prize was a set of six steak knives and forks (very modern, with different coloured handles) and a set of six fish knives and forks, each set in an individual cutlery box. Well, we didn't have much use for the fish knives and forks, but I still have them, whereas the steak knives and forks were very popular and wore out years ago. They were the first steak knives with serrated edges we'd ever seen. In the camps, the men used either their pocketknives, or their big sharp killing knives to cut meat, which was sometimes quite tough.

A good rain filled a nearby water hole in the Woorong Creek, so we went to have a swim when it was hot, with Steven in my arms and Del splashing in the water and loving it. Unfortunately, a dust storm swept down, forcing us to run back to shelter with wet bodies coated with dust, so it was into the shower for us.

We enjoyed living at Mabel Creek with its big staff making it more like a village, with individual married quarters for Don Tanner with his wife and family, Banjo Walkington with his wife and family, and single quarters for Henry O'Toole, Clem, and young Strangways. Together with its big workshops, it was a very-well-equipped station, nothing but the best. With the shearers' quarters well away from the homestead, it was also very quiet.

Marg Rankin and I were the only white women on the place and became good friends; most of the married women of mixed blood were quite shy, but friendly. The mail came once a week with Banjo the mechanic driving the truck to Kingoonya to pick up the mail and loading from the train, and he brought an occasional box of fresh vegetables, which was a real treat.

Del had her second birthday in November and Marg brought her son Chris out to us for a party and cake. Although it was pretty hot, the good fridge meant that we were able to enjoy cold drinks and party food. Chris was about four at the time and called Del 'Cadell' after Johnny Cadell, the country and western singer.

After Del's birthday, the weather started really heating up. The quarters had no power and we experienced one of our hottest summers ever! Ian and Marg invited us into the homestead for Christmas lunch and it was wonderful to eat a delicious meal, with cool drinks, in the air-conditioned dining room. Marg had set the table beautifully, including table napkins. When I mentioned that she was getting a bit flash, at that precise moment two-year-old Del came up to the table and, pointing to the napkins, said 'What's that?' Marg was trying to educate Chris to the niceties of life so he wouldn't ask one day, 'What's that?' at the sight of table napkins. We had a good laugh; the timing was perfect. Ian's parents were staying and were there for lunch too, then after Christmas, all the Rankin's went to Adelaide for the rest of the summer and we looked forward to Colin having a few days off for New Year.

New Year 1960. The mercury went up to 53°C for three days in a row. We were extremely uncomfortable. Colin had three days off for the holiday. All we could do was sit and douse ourselves with water and try to keep cool. Del got prickly heat over her head so I cut off all her hair, which was such a shame as she had soft red curls - which didn't come back. About the coolest place during the day was in the bunker that the Government built to protect people in the event of atomic explosions on Maralinga. We never knew when a bomb was to go off, or how they would let us know anyway!

Mabel Creek Shearer's Quarters and Bunker

Colin rigged up a little swing for Del in the bunker, and it was so hot that the birds couldn't fly; they simply sat on the ground in every bit of shade, gasping and fluttering their wings. Many birds died in that heat; lizards and spiders came into the shelter and stayed quite still. The only water Del could play in (Steven was too small) was the little baby bath, which six-month-old Steven was dunked into a few times. We were fortunate to have a thermometer that rose to the temperatures we were experiencing as most household thermometers only went to 43°C, bursting if they got any hotter. As temperatures were often up to 48°C in those summers, we were glad that we could record the actual figures.

Even higher temperatures occurred during the summer

of 1931, as recorded in Skipper Partridge's biography, *Camel Train and Aeroplane*, Chapter 17, p. 193: *...They arrived at Oodnadatta at 10 p.m. and were puzzled to find the town deserted. They discovered that the entire population of the town was at the dam, for that day the temperature had reached 53°C. One old man, Pat Byrne, had died, and the men of the town had great difficulty digging his grave in the iron hard and burning hot ground. The townspeople told them of the previous six weeks during which the average temperature had been 42°C, and only once had they had a cool spell when it was less than 38°C.*

How well I remember those long hot summers where the night temperature quite often didn't drop below 37°C. In one summer of extended heat around the 47°C mark, we had a cool change to about 40°C, which was quite a relief! At night, we put wire stretchers outside, but it was too hot to sleep when the night temperatures didn't go below 37°C. So we lay there perspiring on hot bedding with Del climbing all over us as we tried to keep ourselves covered with wet napkins. Fortunately, six-month old Steven was able to sleep in his cot in his bedroom, covered with a damp cloth. In fact, he seemed to cope with the heat better than the rest of us.

One night when we were outside looking at the stars and trying to get Del to sleep, I said to Colin, 'Look at that, there's a black line across the stars and they've gone out.' Colin yelled 'dust storm', and I rushed along the veranda to shut all the doors and windows, before we dived under the sheets and pulled them up tight over our heads while the dust storm raged. When it stopped, the sheets were covered in red sand and dust and we were stickier and sweltered even more. But, fortunately it was slightly cooler, or at least it felt that way. We had come through it all right!

Steven was OK in his cot as not a lot of dust got into his

room, although he had a covering of fine red dust. It was pretty hard trying to sleep during the rest of the night, but seeing as we were all exhausted, we did get some. When I picked Steven up next morning there was an imprint of his body on the white under-sheet and pillow. However, a good wash under the cold-water shower off our bedroom made us feel somewhat refreshed. I also had to wash all the bed linen to remove impregnated dust and sand.

We were so thankful when the cool change arrived after three days, by which time I was preparing to take the children into the homestead, to cool off with the air conditioning, even though Ian and Marg were not there. When they came home, they confirmed that it would have been OK.

Colin went back to boring for water and loved pulling the boring plant behind the old Blitz truck. On those jobs, he stayed away until he either struck water or ran out of food, which could be any length of time.

One day he came home very elated, having drilled over 30 metres in one day; at two dollars for every 30 cm, he earned more in that day than ever before, or since for that matter. Considering his weekly wage at Mt Willoughby was $40 a week, it was very good money for a worker in 1960.

I haven't told you about the two-man lavatory at the quarters - a tin shed closed on three sides with a partition about 65cm in front of the opening, and a single dividing wall. Each section had a wooden bench with a hole perched over a long drop that had fallen in from the back wall, through which a perentie (big lizard) scrambled in and out. Although he couldn't 'reach' anywhere near us, it was a bit scary hearing it, but luckily the children were too small to go there and at last I had a 'civilised' lavatory.

When we lived in the caravan, Bert made Del (and subsequently used by the boys) a portable wooden potty seat which, with its lid down, made a chair for Del to sit up to the table when the tray was folded back. Fortunately, the children were easy to train with their bodily functions, unlike Ian and Marg's second son who spent hours sitting on his little potty seat. We all found training a lot easier than dealing with horrid nappies in hard water, which made it so hard to get clothes clean. Staining was always a problem in hard water before the days of liquid bleach, and the clothes dried very stiff.

One night when Colin was away I awoke to asssshhhh-ing sound that I thought was wind blowing sand onto the veranda. Thinking that I'd better cover the children and close their doors and windows against a dust storm, I swung my legs over the edge of the bed, grabbed the torch and, to my horror I saw a big brown snake gliding along the wall by the head of the bed. Well, to this day I do not remember my feet touching the floor between the bed and the door, but I was outside like a flash, slamming the door behind me and stuffing a towel under it to keep the beast in. No, it wasn't wind I heard!

I spent the rest of the night on a stretcher in another room, before ringing Ian at first light. He said he would be over soon to dispose of it, but he didn't arrive until about 8 o'clock. When we gingerly opened the bedroom door there was no snake! So we quietly crept to the adjoining bathroom and there it was, about 2 m of it, twined up the pole with its head around the shower head. Ian was surprised that it was so big, but managed to dispose of it. We surmised that the snake sensed water in the showerhead and decided to try for a drink.

Another day when Colin was home, Ian called in and we piled into his vehicle to go to one of the turkey-nest dams where there was a cow bogged in the mud. If a beast was badly bogged, it could die and foul the water. Ian needed

Colin's help to get a rope around its horns before he pulled it out gently with the Land Rover, allowing it to extract itself near the edge of the dam. While it lay on the ground recovering, Ian released the rope from its horns, but the cow took fright, jumped to its feet, and charged him. Oh my, didn't Ian run, but fortunately the cow was pretty weak and decided not to pursue him, turning away from the dam to live another day. The men had to keep their eyes on the dams to prevent cattle drowning.

As always, washing Colin's greasy, dusty clothes was a chore but there was a large bench in the big laundry where I could lay the clothes out and scrub with the scrubbing brush to try to get his things clean, even his singlets. Drying clothes was never a problem in the heat and I liked to iron our creased cotton clothes out of self-respect, using the latest Tilley kerosene pressure iron primed with a methylated spirit wick.

Tilley pressure iron Courtesy of the Trigg family, Bungaree, Victoria

The Tilley was very effective, though hot to use in summer, and it was a good day when polyester-cotton blends made for easy-care clothing that required little or no ironing.

The children were good during that hot summer, playing on the veranda with Del enjoying pushing Steve along in the meat-safe cot on wheels, which he also enjoyed.

I occasionally rang Marg at the homestead for a bit of company as all the Rankin properties were on a private party line. There was Mr Rankin Snr and his three sons, who each owned a sheep station in a line along the road from McDouall Peak - The Twins, Ingomar, and Mabel Creek. They bought the stations when the price of wool went through the roof and they did very well.

With winter and shearing on the horizon, Ian prepared to build us a cottage near the homestead because the shearers needed their quarters. He got builders to pour the concrete floor and walls for four rooms – kitchen, lounge and two bedrooms – with a veranda all around. Luxury of luxuries, it had a press-button water toilet on the back veranda, and a small wood-burning stove in the kitchen. We moved in as soon as it was habitable, then my parents and sister visited us in their caravan – which was very bold of Dad to drive his Holden sedan towing a caravan over the 650km of dirt road from Port Augusta.

Mustering required a big staff and a camp cook – Don Tanner's wife. Ian bought a red double decker London bus, quite a sight in Central Australia, which became the cook's quarters upstairs, and the kitchen and eating area downstairs. We visited occasionally and it was wonderful to see a proper kitchen, with port-a-gas stove, and kitted out so everyone could eat in shelter away from the flies. I learnt many tips from Don's wife, which proved very useful for cooking on my new wood stove. I had moved past camp cooking.

We had a good relationship with Marg and Ian. At times when Marg was away I gave Ian a hand with visitors to the station and also had use of the homestead electric washing machine - a huge improvement on the hand machine and hand-scrubbing that I had in camp and at the quarters. Being able to hang the washing on a proper clothesline also made life a lot easier. Colin was wonderful, always providing me with whatever improvements he could in camp, but mindful that the camps were only temporary. It wasn't worth spending too much time on extras that had to be set up, dismantled, loaded, unloaded, and set up again with each move.

One day a big covered truck turned up at the station carrying an Afghan hawker with a truck full of wares, which the station hands loved. The hawker had new shirts, hats, boots, drill trousers, socks, sweets and many other goodies for the men, as well as items to delight the hearts of women who bought all manner of bright ribbons, dresses, beads, bangles, frills, furbelows and other items.

The hawker was the gentlest of men and very persuasive. One side of the truck lifted up to make a shady awning with a drop-down, narrow counter. Selected items were beautifully displayed in compartments and drawers inside the truck, including bolts of cloth suitable for making dresses, although some of the materials were quite old with black and white patterns of very small flowers dotted here and there – probably more suited to mourning clothes for earlier times. The hawker didn't go further north beyond the dingo fence grid, where the large cattle stations had less staff and were too far apart to make it profitable.

About the time our cottage was getting near to finished, Mt Willoughby came onto the market because Mrs Brown's son-in-law and manager was very sick with heart trouble and wasn't able to run the station any longer. In fact, he passed away after they left the bush. The Rankin family decided to buy it, seeing that its southern boundary, the dingo fence, was also the northern boundary for Mabel

Creek. Being the successful buyers meant that they had to reorganise various staff; Bill Fleming went to manage Arckaringa and Brad Russell to live on Welbourne Hill. Brad had been on Mt Willoughby and Welbourne Hill all his life and was good mates with Colin, Ernie, Peter Giles from Wintinna, and Bill who had grown up on Mt Willoughby. All of them were strong, young men about 30 years old. Colin got the job of managing the 5000km² Mt Willoughby cattle station.

We only stayed at Mabel Creek for about a year. After we left, our cottage became the schoolhouse and later the teacher's quarters when a larger schoolhouse was built nearby to cater for the increasing numbers of young children on the station. Our next move was to the huge, rambling old homestead at Mt Willoughby – called 'government house'.

Mt Willoughby cattle station was located 257km north of Coober Pedy, 215km west of Oodnadatta, 1,130km north of Adelaide, and 600km south of Alice Springs. Westward, there was only the Woomera Rocket Range (Maralinga), but no roads in that direction. From its southern boundary, the dingo fence, it was 100km to its northern boundary at Wintinna. The Stuart Highway ran through the centre of the property - usual in those days of very few fences where the highway followed the original tracks from homestead to homestead. Mabel Creek Station was west of the Stuart Highway, Mt Clarence on the east, and Coober Pedy on the highway. Gradually the country was changing – there was a great increase in the population of Coober Pedy where most people lived underground, but more dwellings were appearing above ground as opal mining became more popular.

In 1955, Len Beadell started opening up country to the west and north-west from Alice Springs with the Gunbarrel Highway, which wasn't as straight as the name would indicate, or as he would have liked, but the terrain dictated where the road could actually go. He and the Gunbarrel Road Construction Party bulldozed and graded their way into Western Australia while the Stuart Highway, north and south, was being used more and more. Len occasionally called into Willoughby on his way north.

PART III

THE MISSUS

Mt Willoughby Again 1960 - 1965

A new season of life had begun! Back to the north and Mt Willoughby we went with our belongings, such as they were, to settle into the big, rambling, homestead. Returning to Mt Willoughby was such a thrill for Colin as he worked there for twelve years before we went to live at Mabel Creek. His heart was there.

Homestead facing the road – kitchen Breezaire on left next to the chimney. Johnny Lander in front.

As the departing managers said that they were taking all of their furniture, we bought a bedroom suite and a bit of other furniture while we were in Adelaide, only to find they'd left nearly everything in the house which made us think that we'd spent our money for nothing. Eventually, everything turned out OK because we used our new bedroom suite and put the other items in the sunroom for visitors. Mrs Brown's room, being furnished much more elegantly, was used for special visitors.

By this time, Peter and Norma Giles had settled in at Wintinna Station with their growing family, about 30 km north; while Hugh and Laurel Frahn were developing Copper Hills, east of Willoughby, in a variety of bough sheds and caravan while Hugh was getting on with building the rammed earth walls of their future house. Laurel adopted a baby camel that hung around the back door and cried all the time, which would have driven me mad, but Laurel was very patient - I don't know what eventually happened to it. Dick Holt over at Evelyn Downs had married Meredith Lockyer, who had children of her own. Dick's daughter, Louise, was in boarding school in Adelaide and home for holidays, while son Ross, who was still only a young boy, was being educated at the station.

As Norma and I both had young children, we started employing housemaids to help look after them and do the housework. Besides being the 'missus', I was also the station cook. Fortunately or not, depending on one's opinion, at that time Dr Spock's book was promoted as the ultimate guide for young mums with children. I acquired it and read it avidly for more information on how to deal with young children.

Geraldine and Will

Our first housemaid, Geraldine, was employed through the stock agents in Adelaide and travelled on the Ghan from Adelaide to Oodnadatta, where we picked her up. Although she did the work well enough, she was full of gossip about the people in her hometown on Eyre Peninsula and it wasn't long before she took a swag outside to sleep.

One day a middle-aged bloke, Will West, drove in looking for work and Colin gave him a job as cowboy/rouseabout to look after the garden and odd jobs about the house, yards and sheds. He and Geraldine struck up a friendship and in their time off they drove to Copper Hills to visit Hugh and Laurel. Whatever they gossiped about, they really soured our friendship with the Frahns and eventually both Will and Geraldine had to leave, Geraldine with some of my bits and pieces in her suitcase. I don't suppose I'll ever know what she took, but I recall some of the small treasures I missed. When she got to Oodnadatta she didn't get on the first train south, but spent some time in the town.

Government House

There was always time between the departure and arrival of household help, which made life difficult. I was cooking for perhaps half a dozen men and the 'government house' family (us), besides looking after the children and maintaining the big, rambling, house. When we moved in, the breezeway had fly-wire protection against flies and mosquitoes, but no glass windows. Therefore, when the wind blew it filled the house with dust and sand, depending on the severity of the wind, so Colin installed glass louvres, which reduced the dust but didn't eliminate it entirely. However, the end doors still only had fly wire with canvas blinds on the top half, which didn't keep out the dust.

We had two Breezaires for cooling - one in the kitchen, the other in the dining room. Using electricity generated by the lighting plant, they consisted of a large round drum covered with coconut fibre, which rotated through a shallow trough of water while a fan blew air through the drum to cool it by evaporation. A down side was that it raised the humidity.

The Breezaire in the inner dining room was at floor level and worked well for small groups and short stays, but the air became very humid if a large group was having a meal, when in no time they were sweating.

Unfortunately, water from the saturated fibre dripped

onto the fan, which spat it into the room and stained the floor with mineral deposits from the bore water that had to be hand-cleaned by scrubbing with kerosene – such a laborious job. Mopping alone just didn't do the trick.

The kitchen Breezaire was about 90 cm off the floor and didn't really make much difference to the room temperature, except when you were standing directly in front of it. Unfortunately, there wasn't much time to stand still when the kitchen was a hive of industry most days when the men were home. Besides, the bread-cutting machine was on a small table in front of it.

When mice were bad we watched them come out and nibble crumbs on the bread table, so Dad sent us some mouse-traps that could catch four at a time – very handy, very effective, and they got lots of use. We threw the dead mice out the back door where a big perentie (lizard) snatched them, along with other scraps of meat and fat. The perentie stayed for months before disappearing, never to return, which pleased the crows to have those tid-bits.

The kitchen had a small pantry on one side, and a massive four-oven AGA cooker on the opposite side fuelled with coke, which generated a sooty cloud when being filled through a hole in the top. A huge pile of coke outside the back door, but beyond the covered veranda, was topped up by the truckload when required, causing a large cloud of black dust. The stove burnt non-stop because it was a horror to start. Consequently, the kitchen was warm in winter, hot for a few months, then stinking hot from November to March.

Because I was tall, Colin raised the height of the Laminex kitchen table to make it easier for me to knead bread and prepare food without bending over, although its metal edges burned my legs below my shorts in summer.

An old-fashioned wooden table would have been much more user friendly!

The dining room had a huge, but much neglected, polished wooden table that I took delight to restore, polish, and keep looking good. I loved that table because it had lots of space to utilise some of our special wedding presents of silver, crystal, and dinner-ware when we had visitors and special occasions. I liked to set candelabra on the table, but the first time I put candles in it during the heat of summer, the candles melted and bent right over – a comical sight, never repeated.

Although we had three kerosene fridges in the breezeway next to the kitchen, they were virtually useless in summer for anything except keeping food cool – oh, how I longed for the efficient old fridge from the Mabel Creek shearers' quarters, which even made ice in summer. Regrettably, the modern fridges wouldn't even make ice in the 'ice' trays, and if you tried it reduced the capacity for keeping food cool. So it was a no go! The only coolish water was from the water bag at the other end of the breezeway, well away from the hot stove. Who likes the taste of water from a waterbag? Not me, so I learned to drink 'not cool' water.

Helen

Helen Anderson, our next housemaid, flew up from Adelaide to Oodnadatta, where we picked her up. Helen stayed with us for well over two years and eventually became Del's first governess, supervising correspondence schooling and half an hour of School of the Air once a week. She loved spending time sitting on the horse-yard fence with Del when the men were breaking in new colts – something we all enjoyed as it was quite an exciting spectacle, with lots of buck-jumping and other horsey dangers and delights.

Billy on a colt

Horse Breaking

Horse mustering, selecting, and breaking went on periodically in the homestead yards and we loved escaping the housework and cooking to go and watch the excitement. There were plenty of brumbies in the bush, which the men rounded up and herded into the small yard near the house to select the ones suitable for stock or pack horses. Those selected were taken to the breaking yards across the creek from the house; the others were let loose. Because cattle stations had let well-bred horses loose all over central Australia at various times, cross breeding had produced some nice-looking, good-tempered, horses to choose from.

When Del was very little and the men had horses in the little yard next to the tack room, I walked down to watch and there was my little girl – she had slipped under the bottom rail and was walking amongst the horses, patting their legs and saying 'Dear horsy'. I'm sure that if one of the men had been so foolish they would have been kicked, but the horses didn't pay any attention to the little girl. So

I just quietly called 'Come to Mummy Del,' and fortunately she came back under the rail and into Mum's arms – no harm done. Now that was a scary moment.

The children loved the horses and we had a quiet one called Harnomy that they liked to ride. On one occasion, they got on together and Harnomy walked along, then ran down a little washaway and up the other side; the children went sideways, one after the other down to the ground, only to get up and mount again, laughing at such fun.

Horse breaking went on for a couple of weeks and after the colts were quietened the men rode out together to educate them for an hour or two. Sometimes I accompanied them on a quiet horse called Blackie, although I didn't get a lot of opportunities because there was always too much to do at the house.

Dust Storms

It was a busy life at Willoughby - a huge house to maintain and men to cook for, dust storms too often in the summer, three or four a week, sometimes two in a day. Even with the house closed down as much we could, the air was thick with dust. When there was a big dust storm during the night, you sweltered under the sheets while it passed, then got up to find that the only white sheet was under your body; the rest was rusty red.

One night, even though I was in my inner bedroom, I awoke to the sound of raging wind and dust in the air like fog. Although it was so hot, there was only one thing to do – put my head under the sheet and swelter; at least that air wasn't filled with dust. Leaving doors and windows open in such dusty conditions wasn't an option, but when a storm passed it was time to open the doors and windows to let fresh air in, then wait for morning to do the cleaning up.

After a wild storm one night when the children were

very little, I had to shut them in their bedroom in the morning to play, while I shovelled buckets full of sand from the breezeway before letting them loose. Otherwise, they would have scattered sand all through the bedrooms. As it was, they loved running through and kicking the residual sand before I washed the floor. Many dust storms came with a north wind and took hours to clear up, followed by a cool southerly change on the same day that covered us with dust again. The dust got into every nook and cranny of the old house.

To make matters worse, the breezeway consisted of horizontal sheets of corrugated iron, which were wonderful for trapping dust and spider webs. Red back spiders were a fact-of-life; they were everywhere. However, to my knowledge, no one was bitten and they were ignored. They were under every canvas chair in the smoko veranda but if we didn't bother them, they didn't bother us. Of course, all the cobwebs were visible when covered in dust after every dust storm, but I ignored them 'till Christmas time and after summer, when we'd get stuck into extra house cleaning.

Sometimes when a thunderstorm generated a dusty wind but was only accompanied by a few drops of rain, the house became freckled with spots of mud, because there wasn't enough water to wash them off. Nothing could be done; we just accepted it!

Historically, heat and dust weren't new to the area, as demonstrated in an excerpt from 'South Australian History, Oodnadatta town, 1919': *Night brought no relief from the heat, for a hot wind was blowing as from a furnace. The wind was as if it came straight from a super-heated blast furnace and was accompanied by clouds of red dust that filtered through every crevice and covered everything inside and out with a red layer. There has been no rain to speak of at Oodnadatta for two and a half years and the country is absolutely bare.*

Sometimes a little wind suddenly whipped up a swirling willy-willy that produced red stains on wet washing that had just gone onto the line, and those stains didn't come out of the sheets until years after we left the bush. A good thing though, was that once the washing was out, it took only a few minutes to become bone dry – therefore, it could be back inside, folded and put away, before the next load was ready to go out. Fortunately I had an electric washing machine with wringer and good quality bore water.

Bits'n'pieces

On our arrival at Willoughby we inherited some caged canaries whose singing was delightful when we passed them on our way to the toilet. However, all of a sudden, the birds started disappearing and we wondered why. So I sat out there quietly until one day I saw it – a small brown snake coming through the wire. Sneaky thing, but not to worry; I went and got my trusty .22 rifle and shot it. End of snake, but regrettably not before all of the birds had gone. Oh well, we were pretty fatalistic and had no idea how to procure more birds.

There was also a little play house up the path from the birdcage that had been made for Marie, Mrs Brown's granddaughter, when she was a little girl. One day I heard smashing noises which, on investigation, I found my darling daughter and son demolishing the playhouse with a couple of hammers they'd found in the big shed. Seemed strange, but I decided to finish the job and completely demolished it. I don't think it was a great loss because, for reasons unknown, Del didn't like it. In fact neither child was really keen on playing houses; they preferred to be out with the horses, exploring the rubbish dump, walking to the woolshed, or any number of other adventures - they were always occupied!

One day the children came into the house with Steven displaying strange burns on his hand and wrist, which I put under running water to wash it clean. I hadn't a clue what that was about but when they said they'd found a bottle of something in one of the abandoned vehicles at the dump, I sent them back to bring it to me. It was quite a small bottle with tiny writing on the label, so I sniffed and sniffed, trying to determine what it might be. I had never heard of marine adhesive. When his arm stopped burning I put some mercurochrome on it (Auntie Di's red) and it healed up in no time. However, as a result of that little expedition to the tip and my subsequent sniffing of the substance, my lungs got damaged – felt like they were bleeding inside.

So I took off for Oodnadatta to visit the doctor next time he was in town, only to be told that it was my fault for sniffing a bottle that was clearly labelled dangerous and never to breathe it in. I was suitably dismissed by the doctor, but the damage lasted for a years until my lungs finally got better in the altitude and clean air in southern Victoria.

Travellers

Another day a small Kombie van was travelling north, with five older ladies and a young bloke driving, when it broke down at the station. Most city folk had no notion of the roughness of that stony highway or the suitability of the vehicles that they were travelling in, especially for long trips. Usually, there were very few four-wheel-drive vehicles, apart from our station Land Rovers, and Kombie vans and sedan cars were very vulnerable in those extreme road conditions, especially as we were 800km north of the last bitumen at Port Augusta, which didn't start again until Alice Springs.

Therefore the breakdown finished their trip north by road; there was no hope of the group travelling on as major repairs were needed to the vehicle. So we got on the transceiver to see what help was available and as we didn't have suitable transport to take them into Oodna, we contacted Jack Hanney who said he'd come out and pick them up and take them to the train - the only way they'd be able to get back to Adelaide. As these arrangements took a little time, we bedded them all down and fed them for a few days. An experience for everyone concerned!

Travellers calling in for petrol were the bane of my life; we were not set up for supplying petrol to the public. Besides, it cost a lot of money and time to get petrol to the station and into the underground storage – it was a 430km round trip for the truck to pick up a load of 200-litre drums from the Oodnadatta railhead. Before that, they had to be ordered from Adelaide and sent to Oodna! It was also a rough, bush track over stony plains, gypsum plains, and sandy or stony creek beds - quite an expensive, time-consuming task.

Because the road (Stuart Highway) came right past the house, travellers called in without a thought, not that there were many of them in those early days, but enough to be a nuisance. If anyone was absolutely desperate, I charged them 85 cents for four litres when the going price in the city was 25 cents for the same quantity. If they were desperate they were willing to pay, otherwise they had to decide whether they would go on. For us it was an interruption to our mostly very busy life in the house. It also required using a hand pump to raise the petrol into a glass measuring-tank, before letting it flow through a hose into the car's fuel inlet. And we could not risk draining all the station supplies on travellers' wants, especially as they'd been warned at both

Coober Pedy (south) and Kulgera (north) that the cattle stations did not supply petrol.

The road gang (Highways Department) from Oodnadatta constantly patrolled the district roads, grading them when necessary; rain or breakdowns were the only things that stopped them. The men camped wherever they were working, and eventually Colin organised them to grade a new road well away from the homestead and cattle yards so that the dust and visitors didn't bother us so much – but there was a problem! The new road cut through a patch of very soft ground, called bull-dust, where cars could get bogged.

Some travellers got wise and could identify bull-dust patches by the huge amounts of dust that had been thrown onto the surrounding foliage of trees and bushes, and they responded by being wary and driving through the hazard carefully. As the edges of bull-dust patches were very rough, vehicles could fall off the hard road base and get stuck, being unable to either drive forward or reverse out. In that event, the travellers called at the homestead to find someone to pull them out. Usually there was someone home to get a cable and Land Rover to pull them through or, if there were no trees, to tow them around a detour.

Bull-dust, being a fine talc-like powder, shimmered and settled at the same level as the road edges after a vehicle had gone through, so it was difficult to see. However, wise eyes could understand the signs - no wheel tracks and dust over the foliage - but that only came with experience!

Daily Life and Holidays

Helen was a great help in the house and helped me with the bread making, even kneading the loaves with both hands – which I couldn't do. We both got stuck into whatever needed to be done and when we finished our work we sat down and relaxed, or went to the stockyards to see the horses being worked. When the men were home it was constant work preparing and serving them meals and cleaning up, not forgetting the baking for their morning and afternoon smokos.

At Christmas, 1960, I was pregnant again and feeling terrible, but there was nothing that could be done about that. Helen flew down from Oodnadatta and we drove to Adelaide for Christmas and a holiday with the family. In January we traded in the Chev ute for a new Holden wagon that made travelling much more comfortable; we laid the back seats down and covered them with cases, then blankets and pillows to give the children a great place to play or sleep on long trips - all of our trips were long!

In Adelaide, we stayed with Colin's Dad and Mum who had a much larger house than my parents, and we spent time with Ray, Val and their three children, Peter, Ann and Jill. By then my cousins were also having children, so when we got together there was quite a crowd. All the friends I'd grown up with were also married and having families.

After the holidays, we went back to the station, much more comfortably in the wagon, to face the new year. We picked up Helen, who had flown to Oodnadatta.

Visitors

My Dad came on the train to visit whenever he could; as well as friends I'd known all my life who enjoyed the experience of cattle station life. However, as Mother was working, she never came to Mt Willoughby. One of my cousins also came with her husband and baby son, who unfortunately got croup. We contacted the doctor at the base on the next medical sked, and he prescribed antibiotics, which we had in 'the kit' and the little one recovered very well. As he had never had croup before or afterwards, it was a one-off experience for all of us.

Jeff Carter, photographer and author, together with his partner Mare, were other callers I remember. They were touring 'The Centre' to take photographs of bush life, which Jeff published in a beautiful coffee-table book, *Outback in Focus*, printed by Rigby in 1968. There he mentions the degradation of the country caused by hard-hoofed animals on country that had previously only supported kangaroos, emus, lizards, and native people who looked after it so well. By the 1960s, the country looked very different to that experienced by the pioneers 50 to 80 years earlier.

Visitors continued, a great favourite being Catholic priest, Father Bill Wauchope, on his annual circuit. His was a large parish and he always arrived in casual clothes and stayed overnight. Over lunch and dinner, he filled us in on events in the wider district, displaying his great sense of humour - we enjoyed his company immensely. After dinner, he set up his portable altar in the lounge room and invited any Catholics on the place to attend when he held Mass in his church robes, which our people greatly appreciated.

Len Beadell was another who occasionally visited when he was going north by road to his camp. He was also very entertaining but only stayed for smoko or lunch, as time dictated. We were particularly intrigued by his tales of the Gunbarrel Highway heading west from Alice Springs and later about other highways in Western Australia.

An Anglican minister who only came once in the years we were in residence was quite critical of the religious education our children were receiving, which consisted mainly of Sunday School lessons mailed from Adelaide – simple stories of Jesus and the old testament characters that I taught the children. He went away quite disgruntled, despite the fact that Colin and I both had a deep faith in

God which we didn't want to discuss with a man who I am sure thought we were all heathens. He was very different from Flynn and Partridge who ministered by action, not condemnation.

We also had frequent visits by station people from up north going through to Adelaide by road: including the Smiths of Tieyon and New Crown, Doug Fuller from DeRose Hill, the Lowes from Kenmore Park, and Coulthards of Kulgera. We also knew of the Clarkes from Andado and were sad when their son had a serious accident, which many people heard about over the transceiver. We knew their call signs, names, and voices, but never met them, like the folk on the Birdsville and Strzelecki Track stations, right down south to Kevin Rasheed at Wilpena Pound – all connected to the RFDS base at Port Augusta. Stations near the Northern Territory border connected to the Alice Springs base.

Third baby

When I was ready to have my third baby, the children, Helen and I flew to Adelaide three weeks before the due date in May 1961. Jimmy Anderson, a pensioner, came to the station as cook while we were away. Although he received only a very small wage, plus his board, he was an excellent cook and kept the household well fed. It was also good to know that he would keep the kitchen clean while he was there. So I went away feeling very relieved, unlike in other years when the station hands had the run of the kitchen when we were away on annual holidays. It was always a nightmare returning to a kitchen with the stove covered with grease, dirty walls, and a very dirty floor that took a major clean up to bring them back up to scratch – not a happy thought to anticipate after holidays.

Too often we were recalled from holidays early and I had a pretty good idea of what we would find when we got there.

Leaving the men to their own devices was always fraught with difficulties as they were not particular about looking after the station and the Rankin's didn't pay it any attention while we were away. One year when we arrived home to face the usual clean up, we found that the locks on every door, cupboard, and wardrobe in the house had been forced open in the men's desire to get their hands on whatever grog may have been around. They were disappointed on that score because Colin didn't leave any! More damage to repair.

We paid for Helen's flight to Adelaide because we couldn't leave her at the station on her own. By then Dad, Mother, and Miriam had moved to South Terrace where mother worked next door as the national manager at the Girl Guides HQ and Mother was happy to pay Helen to look after the two children and do her housework while I was in hospital.

Once again, Dad took me to hospital (two days before his birthday) for the birth, which I don't remember because the doctor 'put me out to it'. While I was hoping that the birth would coincide with Dad's birthday, when the time came I just didn't care. As usual, my physical condition was skin and bone, so the doctor put me to sleep to let my body do the work. Fortunately, the labour only lasted six hours and David Shane was born about 9.30 am, looking like a miniature Tiger Kunoth, Charlie Kunoth's son. I got a lot of teasing about that when we returned to the station. Although the doctor thought I was pretty poor, being very thin, I was strong and wiry and, apart from chronic hay fever, occasional asthma, and pretty sore lungs, I had pretty good health.

I was out of hospital in ten days, and two days later went to Bill and Bonny's wedding. Bill was Colin's best friend all through the years until Colin passed away in 2012.

Bonny had been housemaid for Norma at Wintinna; Bill was Mrs Brown's grandson and grew up at Mt Willoughby.

When Mrs Brown sold the property, Bill took over Arckaringa Station when Skipper and Mrs (Gertie) Partridge had just retired, and they lived there for many years after they were married. They bought a farm near Kapunda in South Australia after they sold the property and now live in retirement in Tanunda.

We flew home when Shane was just three weeks old – perhaps it wasn't the wisest thing to do, but with Jimmy cooking, I had time to build up my health and spend time with the new baby, as well as doing household chores and caring for the older children. Things went really well, for a change, because I had enough help in the house. Jimmy was great in the kitchen and kept the children out by giving them a double handful of biscuits, which also gave me an incentive to keep them out of his way as much as possible. Jimmy knew what he was doing!

An Unfriendly Visit

When Shane was just six weeks old the owners paid us a visit for the first time. Naturally, we were glad to see them and thought that the purpose of their visit was to see how we were going and to welcome the new addition to our family. Instead, the owner took Colin into the office and accused him of cooking the books with the station paying for Helen's fares and for helping my mother in Adelaide (the accountant would have negated that), while Mrs accused me, in the lounge room, of daring to have a cook AND a housemaid at the station.

We were both, literally and physically, speechless, stunned at those mean and unfounded accusations. They ignored the fact that, with two toddlers and a new baby, I would have found it very difficult to cook for all the staff; and that I also came home early instead of staying in Adelaide for weeks after Shane was born. Nevertheless, they bundled Jimmy into their car and took him south that very day. Colin and I were both gutted - Colin was one of the most honest men I'd ever known. Station owners must think that everyone is out to rob them.

That was the last day that I breast-fed Shane. I had no one to turn to for advice and no support from any quarter; I had to battle along, feeling terribly hurt and betrayed. I couldn't even talk about it to Ian or Marg at Mabel Creek, because the owners were Ian's parents. They caused huge hurt to both of us, and a rift that never fully healed. We never got an apology, although their accountant must have known that we didn't cheat them.

At least when Shane was a baby the weather was cool and the dust storms had stopped. Helen also gave wonderful support to me at that time and 18 months later, in February 1963, she began schooling Del with correspondence lessons and School of the Air in the office. Sadly, Helen left us when she felt that being both a governess and part-time housemaid was not for her. Oh how I missed her. A new governess had to be found, plus a housemaid to help in the house.

Theresa and Tasia

Theresa Malone was the new governess and she flew to Oodnadatta. What a treasure she was - a gentle, kind country girl from a farm near Jamestown in the north of South Australia. Theresa was also very good company and stayed with us until we all left at the end of 1965.

Our new housemaid was Tasia Kot, a girl from the English midlands who had never been outside her city of birth before her family migrated to Australia by sea a few weeks earlier, when they were allocated a Nissen hut in a migrant hostel in an Adelaide suburb.

Tasia on left, then Theresa, myself, my Dad and Colin, Del and Steven in front

Tasia was only 15 years old when our city stock agents employed her to work for me. She travelled by train to Kingoonya, where the Mabel Creek mechanic, Banjo Walkington, met her before he picked up the loading and the mail. Banjo was a very personable man in his early 30s, but Tasia was shocked, never having seen a native person before. It was a very long drive in the truck next day over dirt roads to Mabel Creek, where they put her to bed overnight before Colin picked her and the mail up in the Land Rover the following day. After that ordeal the poor girl never spoke a word for over a week; she was so absolutely overcome by the size and colour of the country, the length of the trip, the size of our house, the family, the staff, and the dry weather. When she arrived she had lovely, curly, blonde hair, but it wasn't long before the curls disappeared – the dry air had straightened them out!

A week later Dad and my sister Miriam, then 12, and her school friend Meredith, paid us a visit during their school holidays. They had travelled to Oodnadatta on the Ghan, where we picked them up. Dad couldn't get over Tasia's silence and awe of her new surroundings. However, he and the girls brought a new board game, 'Squatter,' which we all played and enjoyed. It was a change from Monopoly, the board game of choice before then, and gave us many good laughs.

Meredith was fascinated with the children's fly veils and took to wearing one. When I first arrived in the bush, children wore green cotton fly veils that were clingy and hot to wear, so I sent for some black tulle to make them stiffer, new veils that were like little helmets and much cooler and more convenient for the children. Del's had little bows on the top, but the boys' were plain. They all had hat-band elastic around the bottom edge that tucked loosely under their chins. The new veils were a great innovation, but they were not fool proof because one morning Shane woke up with two totally bung eyes – obviously fly-bitten. Poor little kid! He looked so pathetic and could hardly see on the first day, but his swelling gradually went down after we applied drops from the medical chest, as well as bathing his eyes in boracic. He then knew why he had to keep his veil on – he didn't want a repeat.

Miriam with Del and Shane wearing fly veils
Meat house in the background

City folk were absolutely amazed at how many flies were actually in that country. When the fly numbers were particularly horrendous, the men in the cattle camp put green leaves onto the campfire to create plenty of smoke, then leant into the smoke to get some relief. The horses' responded by standing nose to tail and swishing their tails over each other's faces, or they came close to the smoky fire to put their heads into the smoke. Sometimes the men lit another smoky fire just for the horses.

We spent Christmas at Willoughby that year then went to Adelaide for February. Theresa and Tasia came with us to spend a month with their families, while we stayed at a friend's holiday cottage at Christies Beach. I enrolled Del into the little local school for two weeks to give her some experience in a classroom.

A month later when it was time to return to the bush, Tasia's family would not let her come with us. It was such a blow as they assured us that she would return. Although most of her clothes were still at the station, her family was adamant – they would not allow her to travel back with us. This was despite my parents being really good to Tasia's parents as new migrants; they assisted them in many ways and gave them a washing machine and other goods to help them settle in Adelaide. Tasia's mother was pregnant and said that she needed her help. There was nothing we could do about it, we could not change her mind.

Steven's Accident

On our way home we travelled pretty well non-stop and went into Mabel Creek to visit Ian and Marg to get the latest news from Willoughby. They had just bought a trampoline for Chris, which was set up on the front veranda. After Chris showed Steven how it worked, Steven had a go. Unfortunately, he bounced right off and scalped his head on the concrete windowsill. Shock. Horror. What to do? We were exhausted and about 600km from Port Augusta and

250km from Oodnadatta. It was very late in the day and there were no radio skeds until the following morning. So Ian and Marg took the little lad into the bathroom where they cleaned the wound, pulled the skin back down, then taped it up with Bandaids. What a kerfuffle.

After recovering from the shock, we headed north to home – well awake by then, although the children slept in the back of the wagon. We arrived home about midnight after our very long trip. Steven recovered very well, but with a large scar in his hairline.

Back at the station, minus housemaid, Theresa and I were extremely busy with everything to be done, on top of the usual work to clean the dirty kitchen after it had been left to the station hands for a month. I simply didn't have time to pack up Tasia's things before we received a letter from her parents threatening to take us to court if we didn't return them. I felt it keenly, having so much to do, even with Theresa's help, and with no cowboy for the outside work. Theresa also had to supervise Del's schoolwork, including half an hour a day on the radio School of the Air with Mrs Cockburn at the base.

Eventually I got Tasia's possessions packed into boxes and sent them to Adelaide. Clearly, her family had no comprehension of our life, even though Tasia obviously would have told them what it was like during her months with us. Fortunately, with the children growing and Theresa's help, I was able to manage the chores on my own and never got another housemaid.

I never saw or heard from any of the girls after they left, except for Theresa, who I met many years later in an Adelaide nursing home where my aunt was staying. Theresa was a carer there and knew Auntie's surname, my maiden name, so when I visited Auntie with my mother she greeted me and spent a few minutes remembering her time at Mt Willoughby.

Community Events

As mentioned earlier, three major events each year attracted the whole district to Oodnadatta: the April annual race meeting; the September fete to raise money for the Australian Inland Mission; and a December Christmas celebration for families. The station women organised almost everything, although some of the town's women were pleased to lend a hand.

The licensees at the pub, Bill Smith and his wife were always very good company, with Bill relating many good stories. One I remember concerned some Government guests for whom he roasted a bush turkey (bustard) as a treat for dinner. When Bill asked his visitors if they enjoyed the wild turkey, they answered sternly: 'A wild turkey – yes, delicious, but we shouldn't be eating wild turkey, they're protected,' to which Bill's classic reply was 'You'd be wild too, if you'd just spent three hours in a hot oven!' The subject was never mentioned again; the evidence had vanished down his visitors' throats!

Jarov and Jindra Pecanek at the store were also good company. I recall a big crowd of us gathering in their lounge room after an event where food and drinks were passed around. Not being a drinker, I helped to serve the food and pour drinks (or rather hand cold stubbies to the men) while someone was playing a guitar. It was a great party where no one got drunk, but all were merry. Strangely, it was later called 'Di's party', but don't ask me why!

Jarov and Jindra were also good with the children and let them wander around their store to select what they wanted, with mum's approval, and booked them up for later payment. On our next Adelaide holiday the children went into Coles, then a popular variety store with goods displayed on sloping counters, where they followed the same procedure - picking up what they thought mum would let them have, waving it in front of the assistant, then wandering off to find mum! They quickly learnt that it wasn't Oodnadatta! However, the shop assistants understood when we explained the circumstances and the children returned the goods. As always, the city folk showed great respect for station people.

The Races

The April race meeting was the main event of the year, with the Oodnadatta Cup on Saturday being the main attraction. As usual, there was great anticipation about which horse from the various stations would win, as well as the women's dress parade. Although Colin wasn't the slightest bit interested and I'd never been to a race meeting in my life before Oodnadatta, we joined in the fun with everyone. Usually the station folk arrived in town on Thursday or Friday to clean up their shacks in preparation for the main influx of families and staff, and to catch up with old friends and talk about coming events. Volunteers cleaned the local hall to prepare for Saturday's Races Ball, including preparations for the live band from Port Augusta that usually played all night. After the races, everyone kicked up their heels and enjoyed the dancing and music - and didn't we raise the dust, even on the washed and waxed floor. The men wore their Cuban-heel RM Williams riding boots, not soft dancing shoes, and during the military two-step, a young bloke's foot came down when my foot was going up and wow! He connected so hard that I limped around for the rest of the weekend. Although there was no immediate bruising, my foot was very swollen and when I got home to Willoughby and soaked it in a good warm bath, it looked bruised and black. But it healed in due course.

The formal presentation of the winner's cup took place at a gymkhana at the racecourse on Sunday.

For such an important event, the station women ordered special dresses from mail-order catalogues sent by Farmer's and David Jones' in Sydney and Myer in Adelaide, three times each year - winter, summer, and Christmas. How we looked forward to those catalogues, poring over them weeks ahead to make selections then ordering in good time for the parcels to arrive before the races. One year when there was nothing particularly outstanding for feeling soft and feminine, about five of us had the same dress, but in different colours! How we all laughed, agreeing that it was the only interesting one.

At the first races ball after we were married, I wore my gorgeous lace wedding dress with the sleeves cut out. In later years, when the wedding dress didn't fit because I was either pregnant or feeding a baby, I sewed some new long dresses. One year it was a long, full-skirted, black and white check dress; I used the leftover material to make Del a dress with red velvet sash and white embroidered collar, which she loved.

Pretty dress and red shoes in Adelaide

One Particular Race Meeting

That year the only available space for our family, including Theresa, was the back veranda at the pub fitted with canvas blinds over fly-wire walls, which was quite pleasant. The weather was uncertain and we anxiously watched a north-south line of black clouds and lightning in the distant west. Fortunately, rain held off during the races, but a torrential downpour flooded the Neales before we could pack up and leave. Needless to say, everyone was anxious to get home to see how much rain their stations received, so some folk chartered a plane. However, after a few successful flights, it broke down and the service stopped. What a disappointment – we had to wait longer before setting out!

As we drove to cross the Neales where there were channels about a mile across, with much trepidation Colin walked out to investigate the driveability and decided that Land Rovers would have no problems and cars should be able to get through. So we formed a convoy and drove slowly, but Brad's sedan stopped and as he got out he accidentally dropped his keys into the muddy water. Well, what a funny sight to see all the blokes, bottoms up, trying to find them when, hooray, someone found them!

After the car started with men pushing from behind, we set off again with no further dramas, except that the slippery road made it a slow trip. Fortunately, we were able to drive straight through, but we were extremely tired by the time we got home. Because we decided to avoid our direct road westward to Mt Willoughby because it had a big gypsum plain that became notoriously sticky after rain, we covered nearly 250km around the northern route that came out between Welbourne Hill and Wintinna onto the Stuart Highway, then south to Willoughby.

Sewing Bits

Having taken my grandmother's heavy Pfaff treadle sewing machine into the bush, I made all manner of clothes for the children and myself, as well as mending Colin's shirts and trousers – an ongoing task because, as mentioned earlier, he was very hard on his clothes. One Christmas I made boys' shirts and shorts for my boys and a neighbours, and similar for the girls but with feminine styling. I loved sewing, which Mother taught me on her machine when I was a little girl. Grandma's machine only did forward stitch – no reverse or buttonholes – so I sewed the buttonholes by hand and got really efficient. Being in the bush, I had to order fabrics weeks in advance, but that didn't stop me making most of the children's clothes and a lot of my own clothes, including a new long dress for each year's races ball.

Whenever I went to Adelaide and did some shopping at Myer, I could book things up on our account regardless of what I spent; when I gave my name and address the staff treated me like a queen – they were so in awe of us station women! The account would be duly posted later and a cheque returned by mail, less 10 per cent if paid by the due date, which was always a bit tricky with the mail only coming once a fortnight.

Myers Adelaide staff were very good - there were times when I needed an outfit for a particular event, saw nothing attractive in their catalogue, and didn't know what else was available. When this happened, I wrote to let them know roughly what I had in mind, with measurements and perhaps colours. About a month later, I would receive a bulky parcel with three options from which I usually chose one and returned the others. The staff who made the selections demonstrated great skill; it was called 'ordering on appro' (approval), with accounts being sent and paid by return mail. I always appreciated their selections; it was a wonderful service.

Royal Flying Doctor Service Fundraiser

September was the community get-together to raise funds for the RFDS Australian Inland Mission. There was always a dance on Saturday evening and I can't recall what else occurred, but everyone was very generous with funds and we raised a lot of money. The main thing was to get together and share time. One year I'd made a new full skirt and during one dance, one of the blokes stepped on the hem and the skirt ripped across about halfway up, leaving me with half a skirt and my petticoat showing! So I ripped it all off and Colin took me back to the shack where I changed into another skirt, then went back to the dance. Everyone thought I would be too embarrassed to go back, but I wasn't about to miss the fun. Colin and I loved dancing and we fitted together beautifully and danced well. When I got home, I repaired the skirt by sewing it back together with bobbles around the 'break'. It worked.

Melbourne Cup Sweep

Each November Bob Kempe of Mt Barry organised a Melbourne Cup sweep. While we weren't at all interested in the Melbourne Cup, everyone contributed to make up the prize money - usually $100 for first, $50 for second, and $25 third prize, with any leftover money from the pool going for the horse which ran LAST. Baby Shane won that once, for the sum total of $6. Lucky Shane!

Christmas Party

For one particular Christmas in Oodnadatta, the townswomen decided to have a fancy dress party for the children, so the station women spent a lot of time and innovation raiding sewing boxes and dress-up clothes, bits'n'pieces of fabric, trims and old hats, to deck out their children. It was so exciting to do something different, but what a shock we had when we arrived at the hall. We kitted our bush kids out in all manner of princess and pirate costumes, courtesy of their mums' imaginations and work, while the town kids wore hired fancy dress costumes from Adelaide, which were brightly coloured in exotic silks and satins. The older station kids were quite aware of the differences and felt very dull and colourless; we thought there should have been separate prizes for the best home-made and hired costumes. The townswomen were quite smug and satisfied - they had out-classed the station women. Oh, the divide between town and bush folk was quite marked. We were willing to be friends with anyone, but the townswomen didn't particularly want to co-operate. We got over it.

Other People

Colin always enjoyed meeting up with Joe Tapp, a district contractor, although he never came to Willoughby to work because we had enough staff with skills to handle most jobs. Johnny Hunter was another person whose company he enjoyed. Johnny had previously worked at Mt Willoughby and married a part-aboriginal lass, Mona and they were a lovely couple with an expanding family based in Oodnadatta. We called Johnny 'Borry' – don't ask me why!

Ironbark Davies from Granite Downs, north of Welbourne Hill, was another well-known identity in the district, but I never met him. He also had a small hotel north of Alice Springs on the Stuart Highway.

Then there was Ernie and Lynda Giles, Peter and Norma, Bill and Bonny – all good friends around our age with young families. It was a good community.

Noisy Neighbours

Crows were a constant pest around the chook yard, where they parked on the covered chook run ready to swoop down to steal eggs if given half a chance when hens laid their eggs outside, when we let them out to scratch. Not only that, but they carked all day – such a mournful sound. If I carried a stick and waved it around when I walked out to the chook run to check for eggs, the crows just sat on the fence and carked at me, even when I held it like a rifle.

One day when I decided to carry the rifle behind my back, they flew off the minute I walked out the door. So I decided to get as cunning as the crows and poked a hole in the corner of the fly-wire door and poked my .22 rifle through it. Bingo. Take aim – pop – crow gone! I hung the dead crow on the chook-run fence and it kept the others away for a while. Crows are the smartest, most cunning birds I know.

Another type of crow around Oodnadatta had a long and mournful cark, quite different to the ones about the homestead.

Galahs were another noisy neighbour that liked to nest down in trees in the watercourse, west of the house. Generally, they were not too bad, but when their nests were full of babies it was another story – the babies screamed all day and nearly drove us nuts. When it was so hot, that noise could really get on one's nerves.

Drought and Water

The weather got drier and drier as the years went on until we were in a full-fledged drought and keeping water up to the cattle became a major task. It took Colin two days to go around all the windmills as there was also a wind drought, which meant that the mills couldn't pump enough water. Every mill had a back-up diesel engine to connect to the bore, which had to be regularly inspected, serviced, and filled with sufficient fuel to pump water to fill the tank. During a drought, cattle fill up with water to process the dry feed that they scrounge within a limited distance from the water points, before they have to return for more water. The inspection round of the mills was essential.

On the huge, isolated stations, where there was no supplementary feeding, the men occasionally chop down mulga branches for the cattle to feed on the leaves, but that was limited at Willoughby, which was on gibber country with few trees. Therefore, the cattle only ate what they could reach beyond the water point.

Sometimes there were thunderstorms, called dry storms that only produced rain in isolated areas, which the cattle could smell and walked long distances to find because of the prospect of finding fresh feed. That was always a problem where there were no boundary fences, because the cattle could travel long distances from water. So there had to be a muster to bring them back to the water before they perished. The only fenced area on Mt Willoughby was the 65km² horse paddock - only a tiny part of the station.

Drama

All the men carried a small container of strychnine powder to poison fresh carcases for dingo bait and one day Colin rushed in with a young bloke who had poisoned himself! He had used his pocketknife blade to do the job, then wiped the blade on his trousers and licked it clean – and got a bit of poison on his tongue, causing considerable distress. I gave him a drink of heavily salted water, which should have made him vomit. No go. I told him to put his fingers down his throat. No go. Then I put my fingers way down his throat. Still no go. He then had a cup of coffee and something to eat and was as right as rain. We were all very relieved!

On two occasions, the police radioed all stations along the highway from Port Augusta to inform everyone that there was an escaped criminal heading north along the road, with instructions for everyone to stay indoors, dogs too, and have a rifle at the ready while keeping a lookout. Nothing happened. There was no criminal. On both occasions, they apprehended the crim a long way down the road. It was a bit of excitement though. The Stuart Highway was the worst place to run from the police because everyone was in touch, both on regular and emergency radio skeds, and cars could be tracked from station to station to help locate and apprehend them quickly, even in those early days.

Branding

Bulls were kept with the herd all the time, usually a couple of bulls at each watering point to service the cows, so calving was quite random and branding, ear-marking and cutting (castrating) happened whenever there were enough calves to 'mark'. Each windmill and large waterhole had a bronco yard close-by so that the cattle could be mustered and yarded fairly easily. Branding was a bit of excitement and eagerly looked forward too, so we all drove out to see the action, sometimes for many kilometres. It was also an opportunity to take some goodies to the men, perhaps biscuits, fruitcake, or fresh bread. We never went anywhere without a full tucker box and drinking water.

Pulling up a calf by hand, Bert Mettam front, Colin at back

Trained bronco horses were very strong and walked quietly into noisy, milling groups of cows and calves to allow the rider to select an unmarked calf and drop a rope around its neck so that the horse could pull it to the bronco peg for branding. While one was being branded, the bronco man looked for another to rope and pull to the peg. We had a great bronco horse at the station, ridden by great bronco men - Fred Rousch in earlier times, then Bill Fleming.

After each calf was roped and pulled to the bronco peg, a stockman threw it onto its side to castrate the males and brand the lot for station identification using a red-hot iron heated on a small fire. Then one ear was marked using clippers with the station brand – the position on the ear denoting the year of birth that the stockmen could identify when it was an adult. On its release, the stockmen made a sport of hopping onto its back while it jumped back to the herd to find its mother.

Sometimes the men roped a small calf themselves and either pulled it to the bronco peg or simply threw it onto the ground to earmark and brand it. There was never a dull moment. It was dusty work to mark 30 or 40 calves at a water point, but satisfying when done. Some quite large male calves, called mickeys, that missed the previous muster, were castrated and branded, hopefully before they were old enough to service cows because they were not suitable sires.

One year Bert Mettam, a travelling saddler who renovated the station's saddles every couple of years, brought his wife and two little boys to stay as long as it took him to do his work, and they took a break to see a branding. Bert thoroughly enjoyed joining the men while the children played together in the dust. It was a treat to have some new playmates.

Cutting Out

With few fences on the stations, cattle from adjoining stations covering a huge area sometimes got mixed, which required a muster to separate them. When this happened, the managers and stockmen mustered a big mob into an open space where every beast was identified from its brand, and relevant stockmen on horseback 'cut out' their own cows, calves and bullocks, to form separate, smaller mobs that were controlled by other stockmen.

This was another exciting time in the life of the station

that we loved going out to watch – any excuse to change the mundane home life, especially activities out at a camp, was worth pursuing!

There were always beasts trying to escape and join another mob, so the men holding the little mobs had to work hard to keep them together. At the end of the day the separated mobs were driven to their home stations, with overnight camps along the way. It was difficult to hold them together and get them to settle down at night in a new camp, when all they wanted was to return to their mates.

The stockmen worked two-hour shifts throughout the night to watch the cattle, circling the mob on horseback and singing all the time to hopefully keep them settled. Some blokes recited poetry or told stories – anything to keep the cattle quiet. Any sudden silence or unusual noise could set them off on a 'rush', (called a stampede in American movies). That meant trouble, which was to be avoided at all costs; they could split up and go in any direction to find the other cattle, meaning another muster to cut out again.

Occasionally when driving to the camp we would see a dingo, then the chase would be on – over stones, through crab-holes, and dodging the scrub - the dingoes were pretty good at evading us, but it was a bit of excitement.

Things Meat

Then there was the matter of killing a bullock to supply meat for house and camp, which required searching through the scrub to find a suitable animal and killing it with a bullet; there were usually no yards in the vicinity and no way of 'catching' a wild bullock. When the beast dropped, the men cut its throat to bleed it out, before skinning and cutting it up. It required great skill to lay the skin on the ground to keep the carcase off the dirt. Back at the camp, one of the men cut foliage and brush to lay the fresh meat on to let it set overnight. Ideally, they found a suitable tree to hang the quarters on.

Most of the meat was heavily dry salted, put into hessian bags to protect it from flies, then laid on fresh foliage and covered with more brush or leafy branches. Heat and humidity were bad news for a fresh kill, so the timing was critical; they never killed animals in humid weather. The men waited for a cool change before making a kill and warned the homestead to be ready to drive out to the camp to pick up welcome fresh meat, including some for salting.

When a bullock was dropped with a bullet there was absolutely no stress to the animal. The alternative of chasing an animal into a yard and penning it caused a lot of stress and tough meat. So we reckoned we were more humane and ate the tenderest meat in Australia. That aside, the Central Australian beef always topped the market prices in Adelaide.

Dinner and breakfast at killing time meant fresh steak, which we enjoyed very much after a diet of salt meat. If the weather was cool enough, a little bit of fresh meat was hung in the meat house, but the majority was dry salted until it looked like old leather, which then had to be reconstituted with two or three soakings in water before it became edible.

'First night meat' was such a treat and everyone ate the extra bits'n'pieces - liver, brains, udnagoorika (intestine) and especially fresh chuck steak, slightly underdone. We always barbequed the steak outside on a plate heated over coals, before eating it on a thick piece of bread or damper to soak up the juices. Salt and pepper were the usual condiments - plus the inevitable tomato sauce.

Theresa declared that she liked her steak overdone, so one evening we gave her a piece on bread with a sharp knife to cut off mouthfuls, plus the usual salt and pepper - which she found was quite delicious. However, when she went inside to get something, she was shocked to see red juices soaked into her bread. Her meat was actually underdone and tender, but she was hooked from then and had her steak the same as the rest of us – underdone – and thought that the bread tasted good too, with all the fresh juices soaked in.

I cooked the tongue in well-seasoned water before I placed it in a meat press until it was cold to provide another treat. I also made pressed brawn from scraps of savoury-cooked meat and gelatine. Variety was so welcome.

I gathered the kidney fat and rendered it in a huge cast-iron boiler on the stove to make dripping for cooking and roasting, with any excess going to the blacksmith shop and tack room to use to grease hobble straps, boots and saddles. It kept the leather flexible and nourished in the dry climate, and waterproofed it against wet weather.

Looking after meat was always concerning. Without adequate refrigeration, I had to cook the fresh meat as soon as possible, by roasting or boiling, then let it cool to use for smoko sandwiches and tea-time meals. The meat-safe in the kitchen stood in tins of water to prevent ants crawling in and ruining the meat, but sometimes, if we were not vigilant, the water dried up and the ants got in. Meat ants are tiny little golden creatures that are very hard to see, even in a line. Sometimes cold roasts from the safe were covered with the little blighters - oh dear, more wasted meat. However, if the ants weren't too bad, they were washed off and the 'boundary ridden' affected areas were cut off so that the rest of the meat could be used. It was a firm reminder of the necessity to be alert and keep water in the tins.

Of course every station bragged that they never killed their own bullocks for meat! It was a running joke, but true, that they only ate their neighbour's bullocks, but it all evened out. The skins were salted and pegged out to stretch and dry, then cut into strips to make greenhide hobble straps or ropes by twisting straps together.

A Pig

One year Bob Kemp sent us a pig from Mt Barry where he had a swamp, called Raspberry Bore, where there were lots of reeds over a large area. The pigs originally came from Queensland, but they went wild and were breeding at Raspberry. Bob occasionally trapped a young one, which is how we got one to fatten. And didn't it get fat! We kept it in a pen and fed it kitchen scraps and grain. When killing day came, Colin got a short trough and filled it with water, then lit a fire underneath to heat it up. When the water was almost boiling he slit the pig's throat to let it bleed, then four men picked it up and dunked it in the almost boiling water so that they could scrape its bristles off with butcher's knives and some of my saucepan lids. What fun they had, anticipating fresh pork. Its fat was four cm thick, even in the drought when our bullocks had no extra fat. We revelled in its fatness and the rendered lard that it provided for use in the roasting pan and for making the best pastry.

Colin set up a smoke room and smoked most of it, drawing on recollections from when he was a boy on the family farm in the Barossa Valley – his grandparents and uncles had their own smoke room and processed all their own meat. Colin remembered the smell of that room and the German sausages hanging from hooks in the kitchen above the stove, from which his grandma cut off a length of sausage as required for a meal. He also said that since then, he had never tasted anything quite as good as grandma's mettwurst.

About the time that we left the bush, at the end of 1965, Ernie (the 'Beak') and Lynda bought and installed a cool room, so the change was coming when meat and other perishables, like butter, cheese and salad veg, could be kept without spoiling.

When the drought got worse and the killers were very lean, I resorted to buying dripping and put about three cups into the roasting pan and those roasts soaked up the fat to improve their texture and flavour.

Silversides were another option, which I cooked in a big boiler for hot meals with onion sauce and mustard, plus the inevitable onions, potatoes, and canned peas or beans. We also used it in cold meals and sandwiches.

Cattle to market

Sending bullocks to market once a year during the winter months to generate income involved a long process of preparation, starting with our hopes for a good rain to grow the right feed to fatten the cattle for the market. Colin would drive around the bores to inspect the condition of the steers, but whatever their condition, they had to be sold. Then he'd order a whole train of cattle trucks to come to Warrina siding, south of Oodnadatta (the original rail head before the line was extended to Oodnadatta) about 170km across country from the station. Then there was a muster to cut out the bullocks into a separate mob, be they in store or fat condition. Droving began with four or five men in camp and their tucker and swags on pack-horses. All of the neighbours were notified about the movement of the cattle across country and in the 1960s, the men had portable transceivers to keep in contact every day.

Condamine horse bell

Life in a droving camp was always busy, but with the mob moving along slowly and feeding on the way, it wasn't difficult. The man chosen to be camp cook went ahead with pack-horses to set up camp in a suitable place, light the fire to boil the billy, and start cooking a hot meal for when the men came in. In camp, after the cattle were settled down for the night and a couple of night horses were tethered; the rest were hobbled and let go to feed. The horses usually stayed fairly close to camp, with one or two carrying a Condamine bell attached to a neck-leather that clanged quietly all night as they moved around.

The men made the hobbles out of greenhide and about 20 cm of chain so that when the leathers were attached above the front hooves, the horses could walk but not trot or run. Each man had three or four work horses to cope with the all-day droving, night watches, and resting periods. It could be quite a mob of horses, depending on the number of cattle and men on the drive.

Each morning, the horse tailer was the first up before piccaninny daylight (about 4 am) to stir the fire and put a billy of water on to heat, while listening intently for horse bells tinkling in the distance. Then, he either walked out to get the mob of about 16 or 20 horses, or he mounted a tethered night horse to ride out and bring them in. Every man on night-watch had a tethered horse for guarding the sleeping cattle. A feed of oats was a great draw for bringing the grazing horses in. While the horse tailer was gone, the other men woke to the call of 'daylight' from the man coming off night watch and then they drank their first cup of tea for the day while the camp cook prepared breakfast.

The sound of hobble chains jingling and horse bells clanging became a familiar sound when the plant of horses came into view. After the men had eaten, they saddled up to attend to the cattle that had already stirred and were quietly setting on their way, feeding as they walked. All of the cattle, horses, and men quickly got into the routine.

It took two to three weeks for four to five men to get the cattle across the 170km to Warrina siding, driving them quietly to let them feed and maintain condition; there were no fences and the country varied from gibber plain, breakaway, and sand hills. Keeping the cattle contented was paramount, as they had to arrive at the siding when the train arrived. There was only a holding/trucking yard and loading ramp to hold them while waiting for the train - the train didn't wait for the cattle! So the whole process had to be very carefully timed. Once the cattle were loaded onto the wagons – an operation co-ordinated with the train driver and the stockmen - the train went to Adelaide market, accompanied by a train-drover to make sure that the cattle were well looked after and in good condition when they got there.

The ride home after trucking took two or three days and it was a relief to have the men home again after the long process of preparing the muster to delivering the cattle safely onto the train. They enjoyed their hot showers and the opportunity to wash their clothes after the dusty trip.

In 1965, Ernie Giles bought a semi-trailer cattle truck to transport cattle to the rail by road - it was the end of an era and the beginning of a new one; we only experienced it once.

Friends

One time when Colin arranged to call on Ernie at Welbourne Hill, I went along with him for the drive up the Stuart Highway, but oh, it was hot. We were in the Land Rover heading north when we met a mate going south. Well, when mates meet in the bush they need to share a beer. As neither of them had any cold beer in the days before effective fridges and eskies, they had to be content with warm beer.

So while I sat on the ground hugging the shade of the Land Rover, they downed their beer, which wasn't just warm, it was hot! I had a taste – ugh – not for me. While I whinged about moving on, the men wouldn't move when there was beer and news to be shared. Eventually, after they got merry, we moved on to enjoy a bit of coolness and company with Ernie, Lynda, and their two small children.

Quite often, when friends called in to the station, the men shared a beer in the smoko veranda. No one bothered with glasses – beer came straight out of the bottles, which were always long necks. On those occasions, I picked up the empties and offered the men nibbles. Once, when there was a bottle next to Colin that still felt cold, I upended it for myself – ugh, it had a drowned cigarette butt in it and I got a mouthful of tobacco as well as the dregs. Never again did I upend a bottle!

When Hugh and Laurel's house was nearing completion, they were so pleased to move out of the caravan and bough sheds, then they adopted twin baby boys to share their new living conditions. What a challenge, but they were thrilled to be parents and were up to it; Laurel was a trained nursing sister.

Norma and I visited each other quite often, being about the same age and having children at the same time. Wintinna was about a 40-minute drive up the Stuart Highway, around a turn-off, and over a creek. Unfortunately, Norma suffered from severe asthma and got very sick. Needing a rest, she would come to Willoughby and go to bed in the best bedroom - which had been Grandma Brown's. For these visits, she always brought a beautiful fine china breakfast setting - tray, plates, cups, saucers, teapot, sugar bowl, and a little milk jug. It was very special and we both appreciated it very much and delighted in its use. After a few days, she usually felt much better and went home again. Bonny looked after her children while she was away.

Once when Norma and I flew to Adelaide for different appointments, we arranged for our governesses, housemaids, and children to be together at Mt Willoughby to give them an opportunity to interact. We chose my house because it was the biggest to bed them all. Unfortunately, to our surprise and dismay, they were very glad when we returned. It must have been an interesting few days! We left Theresa in charge, but I believe that Norma's girl was a bit of a challenge!

Another time when Norma and the children visited, Steven and Rowena were running towards each other in the long breezeway when they collided and knocked each other out. It was Steve's third serious knock on the head: the first time when he fell off the back of his high chair - he had a knack of wriggling out of his harness and sitting up on the back of the chair – the second when he bounced off the trampoline at Mabel Creek; and this was the third time.

It was a bit of a worry, but both children were OK and got over it. Norma's third child, Peta Allison, was hyperactive, so I was very thankful that my children were only lively. I felt tired just looking at Peta climbing all over her mother; she was never still, unless she was asleep.

Occasionally when Norma came over we treated ourselves to special drinks, including our own delicious Advocaat mixed with dry ginger ale and ice, which we enjoyed and relaxed with in lounge room. This was only possible in winter when the fridges produced some ice. Without air conditioning in our vehicles and homes, we tended not to visit during the hot summers.

A Piano

Having been a pianist all my life, I decided to get one. So next time when I was in Adelaide I visited a friend who was a musician and dealer in musical instruments, and he procured one for me. He also showed me how to tune it and gave me the appropriate tool. Because it was a bit risky sending a piano to the bush, he deliberately chose one of modest quality and price. The only trouble was, in that dry climate, it went out of tune immediately, even after I retuned it using the special tool. What a disappointment – there I was with a pile of music, a musician (me), and an out-of- tune piano that I couldn't bear to play because I have an acute ear! So the piano should have stayed in Adelaide.

When we left the bush, I took it back to the dealer in Adelaide who resold it and eventually sent me a cheque, which was very decent of him. Some years later when I was living in Victoria at Glen Pedder, Greendale, my dad gave me a very good piano that had belonged to one of my Aunts. I played that for many years before giving it to my grandsons in Sale, who have also made good use of it.

Christmas at Willoughby

One Christmas Colin and the neighbours decided to have a celebration at Willoughby before going to Adelaide for the holiday in February. Ernie brought an extra fridge, which the men filled with lots of beer and the Rankins sent a turkey as usual. As always, I also made the Christmas cakes and puddings (boiled in calico bags in the big boiler) at the end of September, so they were well matured. We had all the trimmings. Christmas day dawned with a really cool change – and the men were so disappointed because it was far too cold to appreciate lots of cold beer, but we still had a good day with friends who enjoyed the roast turkey, pudding, and cake with all the trimmings.

For another Christmas at the station, some friends in Adelaide, who owned a cherry orchard in the hills, airfreighted a half-case of freshly picked cherries to us. Our mouths were watering at the very thought, but it rained the day before the plane landed and we couldn't get into town to pick them up. What a disappointment for us, but at least some Oodnadatta residents enjoyed their special treat!

Colin often returned home late from his station work. When I heard the squeak of his Land Rover brakes pulling up at the gate, I went out to greet him and hear the news before preparing his meal, no matter how late it was. It was good when it was just the two of us.

When the men were home it was always busy, with lots of cooking for their morning and afternoon smokos, besides breakfast, dinner and tea. Breakfast was always steaks; morning smoko was sandwiches with meat and sauce or chutney; biscuits or fruit cake were for afternoon smoko. Mid-day dinner was always a hot meal, whatever the weather, and tea was a cold meal. Dessert was included with dinner, and there was plenty of bread and jam at every meal. When meals were ready, I rang the bell, a big old iron wheel hub banged with a piece of iron. The sound of the bell couldn't be missed! Although we generally had meals at set times, it was handy to call everyone when the meal was ready to save the men from waiting outside the back door and us worrying about blowflies attacking the meal.

When the men were away mustering, it was very quiet at home and we tended to get bored, especially in the evenings. Although Theresa and I played cards, we even got sick of that and played records or read books. I bought the Readers' Digest Condensed Books and subscribed to The Saturday Evening Post from the United States, which was a great magazine in the times when its covers were classic art by Norman Rockwell. How we loved those covers. We also subscribed to the South Australian Stock and Station Journal to keep abreast of multiple country interests.

Bread

Bread was another trial, or not, depending on circumstances. Flour was ordered by the tonne and came in 25kg calico bags that were stored outside on a raised platform underneath a corrugated iron cover to protect it from mice and rain, but not heat. The legs of the platform were mouse-proofed by nailing about 30 cm of tin tightly around their base to prevent mice getting a grip and climbing up. With flour, as with meat, fresh was best.

Making bread in the summer was difficult because the flour often had weevils, which we sifted out, or weevil worms that we couldn't remove, in which case the whole bag had to be discarded. Weevil-infested flour made very poor quality bread; hot flour mixed with cool water reduced it to body temperature. Therefore, each day's bread was made as early as possible in the morning, and even then, it smelled and tasted less than the best. By late afternoon it had gone sour and ropey and had to be thrown out - it was only edible for breakfast, smoko and lunch. Making daily bread was a chore.

Making bread in the winter was good if we had fresh flour – the loaves behaved themselves, rose wonderfully in the oven, and tasted so good. It also kept for two or three days although, with many eating it, it was a constant job to keep up the supply. Normally we made a batch of four big tins, but if there were men in the camp we'd also send them fresh bread if someone was going there. Otherwise, they usually made their own damper or johnny cakes.

Power

Electricity was generated by a very noisy, diesel, engine in a tin shed, 50m from the house. The engine had to be running to use the vacuum cleaner, washing machine, Breezaires, and the Mixmaster, but batteries could keep the transceiver working. If anything else was drawing a lot of power, the engine had to run, including lights in the house and men's quarters. Sometimes when we had visitors and sat up late, we delayed turning the engine off until about 10 pm, after which the lights gradually got dimmer and dimmer until it was time to turn in before it got dark. It was such a relief when the engine and Breezaires were turned off and quiet descended, even when it was hot.

When there were no men at the homestead, I had to start the engine using a routine that Colin taught me - fill it with fuel, check the oil, then crank it. However, I wasn't strong enough to turn the crank handle and feared a kick-back that could have broken my arm or knocked my teeth out! Instead, I pulled the long drive belt, which presented another challenge - to pull it fast enough to turn the engine over. Needs must be met when there is no alternative!

RFDS Radio

Days in the house were divided into defined times dictated by meals and the radio skeds from Port Augusta, when Graham Pitts reigned supreme as a wonderful and respected base anchor. The men with portable transceivers called us at 7 am '8SPB Portable calling SPB' to let us know where they were working and how everything was going. All the radio calls were on the same frequency as the Port Augusta base and I went into the office at 7 am to listen for local messages for maybe five or 10 minutes, depending on news from the different station camps. At 8 am, the Medical and Telegraphic (telegram) sked from the base took priority over everything else. If there were no calls for medical advice, and telegraphic traffic was waiting at the base, each station was called in turn by their individual call sign, which they had to acknowledge, before anyone could have their turn to either receive or transmit messages. Mt. Willoughby was 8WF (8 William Fox) when we first took over, but it changed to 8SPB (8 Sugar Peter Baker) when the network was updated. School of the Air started its half-hour slots from 9.00 am with Mrs Cockburn, School of the Air Supervisor, until the next sked at 11.00 am.

As already mentioned, the radio at Port Augusta reached far and wide, extending to stations near the Birdsville and Strzelecki tracks, Kevin Rasheed south at Wilpena Pound, and Welbourne Hill and Todmorden Stations near the most northerly points. Further north, the stations were outposts of the Alice Springs' base.

At the mid-day 'galah' session, the local-area women contacted each other for a chat, followed by the 2.00 pm and 4.30 pm skeds. At 6.00 pm, the men reported in again on their portables. In these ways, we all felt very connected to one another and knew everyone else's business, although some people didn't like the cattle market prices coming by telegram.

After we left the bush, telephones became the primary means of communication and the close connection between each other became a thing of the past that was greatly missed. With the radio, there was no way you could feel lonely or lacking for company; the news and neighbours' voices could be heard so often during the day, every day. After we left the centre, I was extremely lonely for a number of years until I got to know my neighbours and joined various local groups in town.

One Sunday an emergency call went through to the base from Anna Creek Station - on Sundays, the radio was always on, but there were no official skeds. The Nunn family was away at Quilpie in Queensland visiting relatives, and a young woman at Anna Creek who was in late pregnancy was apparently going into early labour. As there was no way anyone could get help to her because there'd been rain and all the roads were impassable, we listened in for hours while the doctor at Port Augusta gave advice and kept in touch. Because the lass was home alone, it put everyone on tenterhooks, but thankfully it turned out to be a false alarm. However, it stirred everyone and reinforced how scary that isolation could be, especially when it rained.

The ABC was the only general radio station we could receive during the day, so we had no choice. Mind you, with the RFDS radio skeds, School of the Air, and personal sessions, other programs had a very low priority. In any case, no one would be sitting around waiting to hear them. Good night-time reception meant that we could hear many radio stations from different areas of the world, but even they were not regular, and the signals could fade in and out or just produce static. As the ABC came through pretty well and Elvis Presley was popular at that time, all work stopped when Elvis came on. Helen, in particular, just loved Elvis.

I bought a battery-operated record player with a variety of records including classical, musicals from movies, and some seven-inch records with children's songs and stories, which the children loved. I was brought up to love classical music and in later years my daughter said that I brain washed her to also love some of the classics.

When Colin first went to Mt Willoughby in the 1940s, the station's transceiver was an original Traeger pedal radio, which Mrs Lander had to pedal furiously to get enough power to transmit. Being a big woman, she puffed and panted when she transmitted. Fortunately, by the time we arrived, there was a 25-metre aerial to pick up the signal and a bank of batteries that were kept charged, first by the 'windlight' wind power, and later by the diesel lighting plant, which meant that we were in touch with the outside world.

One day a call came through from Arckaringa, where Bonny had a sick little boy, Michael. Because babies always seemed to get sick in the really hot weather, station houses usually had a Breezaire, or similar, to try and keep cool. I drove the 75km to have a yarn with Bonny and assess the best way to deal with the situation. Between the two of us we were able to comfort the little boy until he was OK. I really think that Bonny simply wanted another woman to talk with and share her concerns. Bill and Bonny had two children, Michael and Elly.

Another time Marg Rankin called from Mabel Creek when her little toddler, Greg, was sick, and I drove the 120km south to visit her - and returned on another occasion when Mary was sick. In reality, all she needed was the company of another woman to talk to her on the spot and share her concern for the children.

Visiting

One day Betty Kempe called Norma and me to invite us to visit her at Macumba. As it was pretty unusual to receive such an invitation, and we both had housemaids to look after our children for two or three days, we were thrilled and said that we'd love to come. John Kempe was the manager of Macumba, a Kidman property about 50km to the northeast of Oodnadatta. We had an enjoyable visit, although I'd just begun a course of contraceptive pills (dosages quite unregulated then) and I felt quite strange.

Another time after the family had visited Oodnadatta, we took the Todmorden road north-west of Oodna and stayed with Doug and Mary Lillecrapp and their young children. It was lovely to visit their home. So often we knew of these places but didn't actually visit them; we only talked on the radio and saw the families in Oodna at one of the annual events. It had not been long since Doug and Mary bought Todmorden from Mollie Breaden, who had been there for many years. Mollie was a single lady, and daughter of Joe Breaden who took up the property in the late 1800s. Mollie ran the property with her nephew, David Gardiner and his wife, before it was sold to the Lillecrapps.

I occasionally drove down to Mabel Creek to visit Marg, a good friend. Our mail and stores came up through Mabel Creek from the train which dropped them off at Kingoonya.

In 1964 Ian started getting family-friendly movie films up from Adelaide, which was a great treat. We occasionally drove down and 'went to the pictures'.

Fireworks on 5th November, Guy Fawkes day, was another event that we went to Mabel Creek for, much to the joy of the children and staff.

RFDS plane

Being a radio outstation linked to the Port Augusta base, 800km away, we only saw the little four-seater Cessna 182 when there was an emergency. When Shane got very sick when he was five months old and wouldn't take any fluids, we rushed him into the sisters in Oodnadatta and left him with them. Mothers were definitely not encouraged to stay with their babies, so with all the responsibilities at the station, we went home. The first thing the sisters did was to pitch out his dummy (it was so unhygienic!), then they found that he was allergic to fats in milk, so they put him on Bonlac non-fat milk powder, supplemented with vitamin drops. After about 10 days he was well enough to come home, where he thrived. At 10 months he was sick again, I've forgotten why, but once again he recovered after a visit to the sisters. They were good at their job!

At 15 months, when he was just walking, he became extremely sick, lost weight alarmingly, and had foul nappies. The poor little lad was suffering badly and after I consulted the doctor on the radio, the plane was sent to fly Shane and me to Port Augusta, calling in at Anna Creek on the way to pick up Connie Nunn and one of her littlies. When we got to Port Augusta Shane was immediately put into hospital, where he was examined and X-rayed and continued to lose weight. Again, the hospital didn't want me around, so I went to Adelaide to stay with my parents until he was discharged about a week later.

Although they hadn't identified the problem by the time I returned to Port Augusta to pick him up, the doctor told me there was nothing more they could do for him; basically they were sending him home to die. When we boarded the Ghan to go home he cried and cried - my poor little pale, skin and bone, baby. Although his crying upset the other passengers, there was nothing I could do for him; he would

159

not be comforted. When we changed trains we settled down in our sleeping compartment and eventually got to sleep. Colin picked us up in Oodna and a few days later when I was rinsing his stinking nappy under the tap, a bent nail dropped out! Within a week his stools were back to normal and he began putting on weight. What a miracle!

When I told the doctor on the medical sked he said that the nail couldn't be seen on the X-ray and they were glad he had recovered. I dreaded the 20-month mark, but nothing happened.

Steve was helping me in the kitchen one day when I was grinding up cold cooked meat in the electric meat grinder to make shepherd's pie for tea. He put his fingers down too far and ground the top off his middle finger. Panic stations. We could see the bone and the shredded skin and flesh. The only good thing was that it happened just before the 4.30 pm sked, so we got on to the doctor immediately and he told us what to do. Clean it, bind it up and give him a penicillin injection from the medical kit, and the RFDS plane would come up the next day. It was too late to come that day.

We comforted Steve, who was about four at the time and, with shaking hands, took the penicillin out of the fridge. It was cold, in a large needle, and was a thick white liquid. Theresa was given the task of injecting the poor little lad because she had some nursing training, but it was very difficult due to the thick substance, combined with the large needle and Steve's protesting. I comforted him then put him down to bed where he slept the night through.

What happened to all that minced meat? I simply tossed out the small amount of bloody bits and covered the rest with potato and no-one was any the wiser.

The Cessna 182 left Port Augusta at daylight and reached the station about 11.00 o'clock, where we boarded and left straight away. Theresa stayed behind to look after the house and cooking and to care for the other children. When we arrived at Port Augusta late in the day (the flight took about five hours each way) an ambulance was waiting. The ambos thought it was a bit 'over the top' when they saw this little boy holding up a bandaged finger, but they took us to the stand-by doctor to examine the damage. When he removed the bandage, very roughly I thought – poor little boy – the finger was not as jagged as we'd seen. The skin had closed over the top, but the doctor decided to put Steve into hospital for a couple of days to make sure there was no infection – and told me basically to go home, which of course was not possible, home being was 800 km away.

Because mothers were definitely not welcome in the hospital I went and stayed at the pub where Nan Nourse was the licensee. She loved looking after outback folk and as there were other bushies in town it wasn't too lonely. One of the blokes loaned me his car to visit Steve in hospital, who recovered well, but had lost the tip of his finger. We returned on the next Ghan to Oodna, where Colin picked us up to take us home, where everything was OK.

Meanwhile Colin had a scalp problem, like cradle cap on a baby, with a very scaly head, which was aggravated by hard water and dust. When he was sick of its itching and unsightly appearance, I cut all his hair off with the hand clippers to relieve the itching.

A week after I removed his hair, his skin and eyes turned bright yellow and his urine was quite dark, like port wine, which was a well-known symptom of hepatitis. So I got onto the medical sked the next morning and told the doctor that Colin had these particular symptoms that I reckoned was hepatitis. Well, you could have thought that the world had blown up – the doctor rounded on me, saying that I had no right to diagnose anything and that he would send the plane ASAP to collect Colin and get him into hospital! Colin

161

was bemoaning the fact that he reckoned if I cut all his hair off something would happen, but I tell you, he looked a ghastly colour and his lack of hair didn't mean a lot. The plane picked up my very sick husband on the same day and took him away; the doctor called me on the sked next morning to confirm that Colin had arrived and that he had hepatitis. Not a surprise!

Colin spent several months in isolation at the Port Augusta hospital with three other blokes who had the same disease, but he looked much better when he was discharged. He returned home on the Ghan a much thinner man, but with his colour and hair restored. During his absence, life continued at the station, but he had a lot of book-work to catch up on and took a while to appraise what was going on and get back into the swing of things. After his illness he didn't do anywhere near as much really hard work, contenting himself with more driving to oversee the property and workers.

That reminds me - early in our marriage Colin had barcoo rot, when his skin broke out into open sores; it was thought to be largely due to a lack of fresh vegetables and fruit, and lack of cleanliness in the camp due to the limited water supply - probably the main cause. At home he'd scrub each sore thoroughly with a little brush and eventually the rot stopped. After his hepatitis episode and much improved diet in hospital, it never returned. Barcoo rot was very prevalent in the early days of white settlement.

Native People

Up to the 1960s, many stations had a large camp of native people where, for every five or six working men, there could be up to sixty people - wives, children, grandparents, uncles and aunties, but the numbers fluctuated according to the tribal movements, particularly 'going walkabout' when the whole lot moved to another gathering place before drifting back again. For those working men and their families, the stations provided meat, flour, tea and sugar for everyone, besides outfitting them in basic clothing. The men were good with stock and some of the women were employed in the homestead to cook, clean, or mind children.

Mt Willoughby, Evelyn Downs, and Arckaringadidn't have native populations during my time in the bush because, sadly, in the mid-60s, the government of the day had decreed changes that made life difficult for both the natives and station owners. The station owners were forced to pay the native stockmen the same wages as their white station hands and they were not allowed to keep the families on site, which wasn't realistic. The native men had no hope of supporting their extended families on wages, especially when their families were forced to relocate. So they migrated into the towns to set up camps and lived on welfare, which they called 'sit down money'.

Stock work had been their purpose in life and they were good at it; they also had great respect for the station families. Having no purpose, their lives degenerated in town - they could no longer gather traditional food to supplement their diet and alcohol and sugary foods and drinks caused disastrous health problems. As a result, there was a huge breakdown in family life in town for which the government had no real solutions; it lacked understanding on how the natives lived, and had no workable plans on how to integrate them into society.

We had two permanent part-indigenous station hands, Billy Cullinan and Brad Russell, who were a great pair who had lived most of their lives on the station. When Colin wanted extra stockmen he went to Coober Pedy and employed three or four young mixed-blood men who had grown up at the mission, and brought them to the station for the duration of a muster. A room in the men's quarters was set aside for them and they slept in swags out on muster like everyone else.

When they came to the homestead to eat, they were extremely shy so the back kitchen was prepared for their meals because they were too shy to join the white stockmen in the main kitchen. If they saw me, they would not come through the back door until I was out of sight and had closed the kitchen door behind me. As the cook, I served the same food for all eating areas - back kitchen, kitchen, and dining room – it was quite a chore to prepare, cook, and serve food to three eating areas.

The native lads were provided with tin plates, enamel mugs, and a wooden dining table covered with linoleum, on which there were pots of tea, bread, jam, milk, sugar and cutlery. The meal was laid out just before the bell was rung and after all the men, black and white, had left the house after their meal, only then did the housemaid and I clean the dining room, kitchen, and back kitchen. Although the native boys had been raised on the mission, we wondered what they had been taught about table manners, because they were very messy. We could never understand what they did, but it took us about 20 minutes to clean up before rinsing and washing the dishes and setting up for the next meal.

There was only a cold-water tap over the kitchen sink, with no hot water on tap. Hot water for dish-washing had to be heated in a bit kettle on the Aga stove, which was very quick, but quite tedious compared with today's methods, especially with mounds of greasy dishes.

At one time we had a visit from an Aboriginal Affairs Officer, who was very officious about how we treated the young men from the mission, but after viewing the eating area and sleeping quarters, he could not fault our treatment of the lads.

Serving up roast meat, vegetables, and gravy, or a casserole stew, for fifteen to twenty people was when the blowflies could really cause trouble; a couple of people had to stand at the table and literally keep waving their arms and hands to stop the blowies settling on the food. It required an eagle eye, with all hands on deck, when the meals were being dished out and placed in the three areas; everyone had to come quickly and sit at the table after the bell was rung. Modern homes are much more securely sealed – not like those old homesteads where the flies had easy access through ill-fitting doors and broken fly-screens.

Sometimes I'd overhear stockmen say things like: 'What's she got for us today?' (that's putting it politely!) which didn't exactly make me feel confident, but over time I got better at making suitable food for hungry men - and there was always plenty of meat.

So cooking was a big task. After we'd shared 'first night meat' we all loved a roast, and I'd cook up a whole shoulder of beef. Sometimes I'd have to trim its length and width to fit it into the huge roasting pan, which was still extremely heavy to get in and out of the oven - but the meat was delicious! Fortunately the Aga had four ovens – two hot and two warming ovens, plus a warming hob; the shoulder took up all the space in the top hot oven. The circular lids over the hot plates were huge, and when they were lifted the heat was enormous, enabling the big kettle to boil quickly. It was almost impossible to adjust the heat in a coke stove – it was hot all the time.

Stews, curries and casseroles were very popular if there was plenty of fresh meat, otherwise we used large quantities of dry salted meat that had to be soaked and heated a couple of times to leach out the salt, then boiled and cooled for cold meat; it wasn't very successful in stews, but could be used if one was desperate.

Vegetables were cooked in roasting pans in the bottom ovens, usually only onions and potatoes. Other fresh vegies were virtually unknown, except an occasional pumpkin and carrots sent from Mabel Creek with the weekly mail. Otherwise, tinned peas and beans were the staple greens. Tinned beetroot was popular with cold roast; chutney and tomato sauce were always available. One station hand ate tomato sauce on EVERYTHING, even bread and jam. I think he had an addiction!

In spring, Colin planted tomatoes, cucumbers and perhaps some pumpkins, but he had to be home to tend them. When the weather got really hot they'd shrivel up and burn. We also had a small lucerne patch in the vegie garden and when we had a milking cow or goat I would go and scythe a row to feed the animal, which was such a treat for them.

Biscuits and cakes were everyday items to cook for smokos and there was plenty of dried fruit in the store (our stores were ordered in cartons by the truckload every six months). Fruit and sultana cakes were also popular, cooked in big deep pans. Also fruity biscuits – something with a 'bit of body'. Summer dessert every day was usually custard, made with powdered milk, sugar, and custard powder, plus canned plums, peaches or apricots. Desiccated coconut or nutmeg were sometimes added for a change; boiled puddings, baked rice-custard, jam tarts, or similar were popular in winter

Rain

The average annual rainfall for the district was about 120mm and if that all fell in one or two events, we got good feed to fatten cattle when it came at the right time of year – succulents such as the fattening winter parakylia and grasses with summer rain. That sort of rain filled the crab holes (shallow depressions that held sweet water for a week or two) and sometimes topped-up waterholes along the creeks – but it was quite variable. In the driest year of my 11 years in the bush we only had 26mm which, had it fallen in a single event, would have grown good feed. But in dribs and drabs it was well-nigh useless and enticed the cattle out from the windmills in search of the fresh rain, which meant a lot of mustering to bring them back for water before they perished.

When it got extremely dry as the drought continued, Colin took to driving way out west, always searching for new places to feed the cattle, but because we were in gibber plain country the cattle couldn't be taken too far from water. We didn't have many kangaroos around the homestead area, but there were a lot further south on the Pooramingie plain. Once, early on, when Colin and I were driving to look at the condition of the cattle, the whole plain was a moving mob of kangaroos, including an albino which Colin saw again.

Sometimes we only got spots of rain in a dust storm that left the house freckled, but at other times there could be wonderful downpours. Once we had heavy rain and the track from Oodnadatta became a roaring torrent of water, like a river, that reached the front doorstep but fortunately fell as quickly as it rose and didn't enter the house. But it overflowed from a roof valley at the junction of two roof lines located over the central back breezeway, soaking the Caneite ceiling and causing it to cave in. Fortunately, there was a small step from the breezeway to the bedrooms, which prevented water from entering the bedrooms. However it was quite a waterfall in the middle of the house, which we sopped up with towels and the mop. An exciting event for the children – a waterfall inside!

For Del's seventh birthday, I invited Norma and the

children over for a party, for which I had already made the cake. Unfortunately we had half an inch of rain during the morning and they couldn't come. It was such a disappointment for the children, but that was life in the bush. We had our own party and enjoyed the cake.

When the creeks overflowed and covered the highway with water, many travellers rashly kept driving without knowing how deep it was. Sometimes when we went to see how the water was flowing in the creek north of the homestead, we stopped many a traveller to tell them to walk through the water to test the depth and strength of the flow before driving through. Talking of travellers, we often chuckled at the number who stopped to get water from the overflowing tank at the bore on the highway, south of the homestead, which supplied Cooper Pedy. Because they had been warned to never drink still water, only running water, they drove past shallow crab-holes with beautiful soft drinking water that formed after a good rain. Had they looked into the top of the tank, they would have seen dozens of drowned budgies and waxbills banked up near the overflow. Oh well, ignorance was bliss. We never heard of anyone dying from drinking that water.

We all rejoiced when there was good rain and our radios were buzzing to find out how much everyone got. The drought officially lasted from 1958 to 1967, when the whole of central Australia had record rains, 36 inches (915mm) in the year, which was unheard of in that country. Lake Eyre filled for the first time in years and the trees and herbage regenerated after many years of being pummelled by cattle, horses, camels, rabbits, and goats. Although many folk said that the flora would never return, with that wonderful rain it did. Unfortunately we were not there to witness it, but we surely heard about it.

Local Outings

Quite often when the men were away I'd take the girls and children out, as there were lots of beautiful places to go to and explore. The Devil's Rockhole, north-east of the homestead, was a favourite place to take family and visitors to pick up coloured chalk stones which the children used to draw on the concrete paths at the house. There were also other interesting stones embedded with fossil sea-shells and other bits'n'pieces. I still have some of those and they make interesting conversation pieces.

Branson's Rock Hole was another good place that held water after rain and was great for the children to climb around on. We also climbed some of the hills to a trig marker on the top which gave a good view of the surrounding country.

Old Mt Willoughby homestead was also an interesting place to visit.

Original Mt Willoughby homestead

Coober Pedy Water

Coober Pedy needed water and one day a couple of young men came to the house in a water tanker to seek permission to take water from our Matherson's bore on the Stuart Highway, about 150km north of Coober Pedy and 45km south of the station. The bore had good water and they were given permission to take two or three loads a week. However, one day they arrived at the station in a traveller's car – their truck had broken down. So we put them up for a few days and messaged the base at Port Augusta to relay information about the breakdown to Coober Pedy, as we had no direct radio communication with Coober Pedy.

Then Colin went and investigated the problem, ordered the parts for delivery in Oodnadatta, drove in to pick up the parts, then repaired the truck to get the lads back on the road again. What a man! About two months later they returned to the homestead and handed me a package which contained a gorgeous doublet opal as thanks for what we did for them. It was a lovely gift, which I had mounted on a bar brooch in Adelaide when we were next there for holidays.

Other Bits

On two separate occasions we attended events in Adelaide with other bush folk; the first was to attend a Glenelg Church for the funeral of Phil Giles, of Welbourne Hill Station, who was Ernie and Peter Giles' father.

The second was for Peta Allison Giles' christening, where Colin and I were god-parents. It was lovely to dress ourselves and the children for the service, then join the family for refreshments later at the house. At photo time the children were not amused - formal dressing wasn't on their usual agenda; they preferred to be outside playing together. However they looked great dressed in their best!

All dressed up but not happy!

On returning home we noticed an increase in the travelling public braving the Stuart Highway, including the number turning up at our door hoping to get petrol, even though the road didn't pass close to the house. However the children loved running out to see them, while they seemed to pity our 'poor little children, with no lollies at a corner shop' and plied them with sweets by the bag-full, much to my annoyance. We had a plain, healthy diet – apart from an absence of fresh fruit – and by then Colin was home more and had an abundant vegetable garden – tomatoes and cucumbers especially

Usually when a strange car pulled up at the gate our big blue cattle dog, Joe, rushed out barking with his hackles up, and the travellers tended to stay in their car. This didn't worry me because Joe was pretty old and toothless, but they didn't know that.

When there was enough feed near the house we had a

milking cow; at another time we had a white Saanen goat called 'Sunshine'. Before then we only had the 'Sunshine' powdered variety of milk. Colin made a stand near the back door for the goat to jump up on when coaxed with a tin of oats, so that I could milk her without having to bend down or sit on a stool. It was great.

With the cow, we had a cream separator near the kitchen door and I did the honours until a young fellow arrived as the new cowboy/rouseabout. As he dearly wanted to do the separating, I demonstrated how to wind it up and adjust the speed to produce the required thickness of cream. Given that it was hard to get going, which I had told him, he grabbed the side of the milk bowl to get purchase and tipped the lot over my woollen tartan kilt and feet. I was not amused and there was NEITHER milk or cream that day!

Milking the cow or goat was strictly a wintertime activity for me because the summers were far too hot and there wasn't enough good feed for the animals to produce milk. In any case, we didn't have decent refrigeration to store it.

Children

One summer the children all had ringworm which we thought they caught from a black kitten, but later found they were from a puppy given to us by Dick and Connie Nunn from Anna Creek. So the kitten and the puppy were banished, and the spots on the children were covered with mercurochrome to dry the sores off. The doctor recommended iodine, but that was too painful and cruel to put on little kids. Del had a large one on the top of her head, so for the second time all her hair had to be cut off. I sewed her some pretty caps, which she'd whip off to show her bald, red, ringworm patch to the travellers and they'd quickly decide to move on and not bother us – after handing over the usual lollies 'for the poor little girl.'

Because it was summer, the ringworms spread like wildfire on their sweaty little bodies. It wasn't an easy time for any of us, them with their itching, and mum trying to stop the cross-infection, but not succeeding. Eventually they dried up and healed when the weather cooled. Mercurochrome was used for all their little cuts and bruises, besides the ringworm; any visiting children wanted some of 'Auntie Di's red' when they got a bump or scratch.

Del had gastroenteritis when she was 11 months old, but since then she was a healthy little girl, very bright and clever. She did the things little girls do – including playing with her dolls and brothers, mostly amicably when they were little.

Steven's life was fairly uneventful, apart from the three bangs on the head, and like all boys he was pretty adventurous.

When Shane was three we decided he needed further investigation because he still wasn't really well, so I made an appointment to see a leading Adelaide paediatrician. How then would we go to Adelaide this time? Well, the bush grapevine did its job and Mona Lowe, from Kenmore Park Station up near the border, offered to pick us up at Willoughby on her drive to Adelaide with one of her children. With all our men away, Theresa was capable of looking after the household and two older children, so I could leave her in charge. Mona duly arrived and we set out in her station wagon to drive and drive and drive non-stop to Adelaide. We did it in 21 hours but we weren't tired, just stimulated with talking and looking after the children. When we arrived in Adelaide very early in the morning she dropped us at my parents' home. Although it was a mutually enjoyable trip, Mona and I never met again - but then that was pretty common for those times and distances.

After seeing the specialist, Shane was admitted to the

Adelaide Children's Hospital in North Adelaide in a ward with about half a dozen other children and babies. He cried bitterly when I left him there, but as usual mothers had to leave and the nurses comforted the little ones who felt so abandoned. He was in hospital for about 10 days and showed great improvement on a different diet that included vitamins and minerals which he was so obviously lacking. After his discharge, we stayed with Dad and Mum for another few days before flying home.

Whenever we were on holidays in Adelaide it was pretty hard on the rest of the family, with the children accustomed to a free life in wide open spaces; they found the city quite confining and we did a lot of visiting. I called them my bush brumbies! Fortunately they have all grown up to be well-balanced, hardworking, responsible adults, which is very pleasing.

One of our visits was to a long-time, part-indigenous friend of Colin, George Tongari and his wife, who lived in a beautifully-kept home with their little children, who were a credit to them. They had left the bush to make a better life in Adelaide, but sadly we eventually lost touch.

Camels

On one trip out bush Colin took Steven camping, when he was four or five years old. As it was hot weather, he took the canvas cover off and folded the Land Rover windscreen down to make it more comfortable driving into the breeze. Along the way they came across some camels, which were quite rare on the station, and Colin decided to shoot one for its meat.

Although it was quite a scary experience for them to be driving alongside half a dozen galloping camels that towered over them, Colin took a shot with his hand gun and downed one, which was very exciting for young Steven. Colin then cut out the fillet steak along the backbone, and removed the hump, which he discovered was all fat. Large humps indicate well-fed camel, and vice versa. After he skinned the hump and cut it into pieces, he placed them into a 200 litre drum and rendered it over a fire to make a wonderful supply of grease for boots, saddles, bridles and hobble straps. The fat was a great supplement to what was normally a very plentiful supply of bullock fat.

Colin hung the camel meat in the meat house for two or three days, wondering if it would be OK to eat, but when it was cut and fried it was tasty and tender – which unfortunately turned out to be a one-off treat because we never saw any more camels.

Troubles

As time went on the drought got worse; cattle numbers had to be reduced and the house meat became dry and tough - there weren't many bullocks suitable for meat and I had to buy dripping to cook the roasts, which the meat literally soaked up.

Then we had a severe sand storm from the west that almost covered parts of the wire fence around the house and turned the lawns into sand dunes. It was quite distressing as I'd spent a lot of time tending and watering that little bit of green, so when Colin and the men returned from camp I asked him if he could spare the men for a day to shovel the sand away - he said no, the men deserved a day off and he wouldn't sanction it! I tried to reason with him - it was far too big a job for me and everyone would benefit from seeing the yard properly maintained. But he wouldn't hear of it, so we lived without lawns after that and I was very upset and hurt!

At that time we were also experiencing the effects of our strained relations with the station's owners, who complained about the money we were spending, despite the fact that they only paid us minimum wages, plus the home and food, which we appreciated. However, we were certainly not the spendthrifts that they implied. Thinking back, the ongoing drought made it tough for everyone.

So, with the children growing up we began to think of our futures, including the costs to send them to boarding school in Adelaide – which we personally could not possibly afford, considering travel costs, school fees, uniforms, tuition, and other ancillary expenses.

I certainly didn't want to separate from my husband, although I knew he loved Mt Willoughby and would like to stay, but he was spending more and more time away from home and I wondered just what sort of life we were all living. All our friends, the two Giles' families, Bill and Bonny, Bob and Rona Kemp, Dick Holt and his family, Doug and Mary Lillecrapp, and the Rankin families all owned their properties. Apart from the Kidman properties, Macumba and Anna Creek that had working managers, we were the only working managers in that area and we simply didn't have the resources to consider future education expenses.

So, with much heartache, we decided to 'call it a day' at the end of 1965, by which time our relationship with the owners was very frosty and barely civil, in spite of our really good relationships with neighbours and friends. We farewelled Theresa at the end of the school year and she flew home to her family in Adelaide.

We set the 31st of December as our departure date, celebrated Christmas at the station, and arranged for a removalist to pick up our furniture and other household items, excluding the meat-safe cot that we no longer needed and sold to a young couple starting a new family at Mt Barry Station.

That year the owners didn't send the usual turkey for

Christmas dinner so it was going to be roast beef until, to our surprise, the cowboy drove out early to check on a bore and came home with a bush turkey that I roasted for a very special Christmas dinner. The men all very generously gave us lovely gifts and we mainly reciprocated with whisky or beer, which they considered a treat because we normally didn't keep alcohol for them.

Straight after Christmas I started to thoroughly clean the house for our handover to the owners – no small task single-handed, especially in the heat with the children running around and family and staff to feed. When I was busy cleaning, the owners arrived and told me not to bother, but it wasn't in my nature to leave a dirty house for people to hear about later.

So, with much heartache on Colin's part, relief on mine, and excitement for the children, we saw our furniture loaded and despatched before setting out on our drive south, calling in to farewell Ian, Marg and their children at Mabel Creek, down the private road to Glen and family at Ingomar, followed by Darryl and family at The Twins before driving onto Woomera where we had permission to go through the government-protected area to Pimba, then Port Augusta and Adelaide to face an uncertain future – but that is a story for another time!

Postscript

After a couple of positions in South Australia and Victoria, Colin was appointed manager of a beautiful, 460 hectare, historic cattle station called Glen Pedder in Greendale, Victoria, in 1970. It was a pleasant change to live in a 'green and pleasant land' that was very cold, very green, and very wet in contrast to the heat, red sand, and drought in the centre.

Glen Pedder historic homestead!

We stayed at Glen Pedder until Colin retired in 1993, then went to Allendale, near Creswick, where he left an amazing legacy in the form of a white, mud-brick house that he and Dianne built themselves. Colin passed away in 2012 and Dianne continues to live in the beautiful home on a hectare of land.

Allendale house

REFERENCES

I am indebted to the following authors – they refreshed memories for my story and opened my understanding of the Australian centre of 50 to 150 years ago:

Ford, Margaret. *Beyond the Furthest Fences* [1966 Rigby]

Grant, Arch. *Camel Train, & Aeroplane, the Story of Skipper Partridge* [1981 Rigby]

Beadell, Len. *Too Long in the Bush* [1965 Weldon Publishing]

Durack, Mary. *Kings in Grass Castles* [1959 Constable & Co.] *Sons in the Saddle* [1983 Corgi]

Fuller, Basil. *The Ghan* [1975 Rigby]

Groom, Arthur. *I Saw a Strange Land – Journeys in Central Australia* [1961 Angus & Robertson]

Hammar, Jacqueline. *Daughter of the Territory* [2015 Allen & Unwin]

Idriess, Ion. *Flynn of the Inland* [1965 Angus & Robertson] *Isles of Despair* [1947 Angus & Robertson] *Cattle King* [1936 Angus & Robertson]

Johannsen, Kurt. *A Son of the Red Centre*, [1992 Ghecko Books]

Marsh, Bill 'Swampy'. *Outback Flying Doctor Stories* [1981 BBC Books] *Great Australian Droving Stories* [2007 ABC Books]

Mountford, Charles P. *Brown Men and Red Sand* [1951 Angus & Robertson]

O'Connor, Elizabeth. *Steak for Breakfast* [1958 Angus & Robertson] *Second Helping* [1961 Angus & Robertson]

Plowman, Bruce. *The Man from Oodnadatta* [1933 Angus & Robertson]

Reynolds, Henry. *With the White People* [1990 Penguin]

Simpson, Bruce. *Where the Outback Drovers Ride* [2005 ABC Books]

Strehlow, Theodor. *Journey to Horseshoe Bend* [1969 Angus & Robertson]

Printed in the United States
By Bookmasters